I0605625

Irish

History & Culture Through Language

LAURA PAKENHAM

ADAMS MEDIA

New York Amsterdam/Antwerp London Toronto
Sydney/Melbourne New Delhi

Adams Media
An Imprint of Simon & Schuster, LLC
100 Technology Center Drive
Stoughton, MA 02072

For more than 100 years, Simon & Schuster has championed authors and the stories they create. By respecting the copyright of an author's intellectual property, you enable Simon & Schuster and the author to continue publishing exceptional books for years to come. We thank you for supporting the author's copyright by purchasing an authorized edition of this book.

No amount of this book may be reproduced or stored in any format, nor may it be uploaded to any website, database, language-learning model, or other repository, retrieval, or artificial intelligence system without express permission. All rights reserved. Inquiries may be directed to Simon & Schuster, 1230 Avenue of the Americas, New York, NY 10020 or permissions@simonandschuster.com.

Copyright © 2026 by Simon & Schuster, LLC.

All rights reserved, including the right to reproduce this book or portions thereof in any form whatsoever. For information, address Adams Media Subsidiary Rights Department, 1230 Avenue of the Americas, New York, NY 10020.

First Adams Media hardcover edition January 2026

ADAMS MEDIA and colophon are registered trademarks of Simon & Schuster, LLC.

Simon & Schuster strongly believes in freedom of expression and stands against censorship in all its forms. For more information, visit BooksBelong.com.

For information about special discounts for bulk purchases, please contact Simon & Schuster Special Sales at 1-866-506-1949 or business@simonandschuster.com.

The Simon & Schuster Speakers Bureau can bring authors to your live event. For more information or to book an event, contact the Simon & Schuster Speakers Bureau at 1-866-248-3049 or visit our website at www.simonspeakers.com.

Interior design by Colleen Cunningham
Interior images © Adobe Stock/Peter Hermes Furian; 123RF/djvstock

Manufactured in the United States of America

1 2025

Library of Congress Control Number: 2025948015

ISBN 978-1-5072-2515-8
ISBN 978-1-5072-2516-5 (ebook)

Many of the designations used by manufacturers and sellers to distinguish their products are claimed as trademarks. Where those designations appear in this book and Simon & Schuster, LLC, was aware of a trademark claim, the designations have been printed with initial capital letters.

To my beautiful parents,
Roibéard agus Clár.
I will forever be grateful to you both for
every ounce of *grá* and support
you have poured into me.

And, to *mo dheartháir*, Roibéard.
Your incredible knowledge and wisdom
amaze me and inspire me every day.
My number one supporter and right-hand man
since day one, and forever and always.

Contents

5. Rituals and Traditions 125

6. Blessings, Curses, and Proverbs 157

7. Idioms and Colloquialisms 203

Introduction

Why say "thanks" when you can say *go raibh maith agat*? Why ask "What's up?" when you could ask *Aon chraic?* or tell a partner "I love you" when you could call them *a chuisle* (that your love for them surges through your veins)?

You'll find each of these Irish words, phrases, and more throughout *Speak the World: Irish*. Using this book, you can easily add a little *Gaeilge*, the Irish language, into your daily life. Not only does this study and practice of these common, beautiful words widen your horizons, but it helps this lively culture flourish even more.

To really understand a country and its people, you need to learn the history of its language. In Chapter 1, you'll discover *Gaeilge*'s history, where the language is today, and where the future of the language stands. Then, Chapter 2 gives a short briefing about Irish pronunciation to help you with common mistakes or confusing parts of the language. (Pronunciation can be tricky, so try to incorporate the words into everyday speech to cement it in your mind!) Then you'll get to the words and phrases themselves!

You'll find five chapters filled with two hundred of the most common, important, and fun words in the Irish language, such as:

- *Beir bua* (best wishes) or *maidin mhaith* (good morning) in Chapter 3: Greetings, Farewells, and Conversations
- *Abú* (hooray) or *céilí* (a social gathering) in Chapter 4: Fun and Entertainment
- *Cáca baile* (soda bread) or *Oíche Shamhna* (Halloween) in Chapter 5: Rituals and Traditions
- And more!

For each word, you'll learn its pronunciation, part of speech, and an English translation of the term. Then, you'll dive into what this term tells you about Irish history and culture, as well as ways to use the phrase for yourself.

As the Irish proverb says, *tír gan teanga, tír gan anam*, or "a country without a language is a country without a soul." So, whether you're interested in learning Irish for an upcoming trip, to connect with your familial heritage, or perhaps to throw a few phrases out over a pint for St. Patrick's Day, the words and cultural lessons in these pages will help you begin to understand the soul of Ireland.

1 Gaeilge's Past, Present, and Future

The Irish language has a long history and its use and status in the country has fluctuated over time. However, Irish cannot be viewed in the same light as dead languages you may think of like Latin or the hieroglyphics of ancient Egypt. *Gaeilge* has been continuously used to communicate since its beginning, and it is still being taught and celebrated even outside of the country. Ireland may be small, but its residents (and those that share even a small bit of Irish blood) are more enthusiastic about *Gaeilge* than ever. In these first pages, you'll learn the history of the past centuries of fighting for the right to speak *Gaeilge* in Ireland, understand the language's growing presence in schools and media today, and consider how the language and culture will grow in the future. From the twelfth century, the language faced challenges; however, the strong sense of Irish determination to preserve their language never faltered. The language is growing and still being fought for even outside of Irish borders.

Gaeilge's Past

The tale of the Irish language is as captivating as those who speak it. What would become the Irish language was first spoken by those who arrived on Irish shores over 2,500 years ago, making it one of the oldest written languages that is still spoken today. Irish was first seen documented in *Ogham (oh-um)* form in the fifth century. *Ogham* is an early medieval alphabet with a system of lines and notches used to represent the sounds of the Irish language. Today, this version of the language can still be found preserved on over four hundred surviving stone monuments, suggesting a deep appreciation of literary achievement.

Challenges Against *Gaeilge*

In 1169, Anglo-Norman conquerors on behalf of the English crown were invited to Ireland by King Diarmuid Mac Murchada to help fight a feud against the High King of Ireland. Afterward, the Anglo-Normans remained on the island and gradually assimilated over the next two hundred years, even adding some of their own words into the Irish language, such as *garsún* (boy).

The presence of the English crown in Ireland remained for the next four centuries and their conquests continued. Irish music, language, culture, and traditions were outlawed through English legislation. Article Three of the Statute of Kilkenny forbade the Irish people from speaking *Gaeilge* to and with English colonists. The Penal Laws of the seventeenth to the nineteenth centuries, introduced by King William of Orange, were a collection of laws specifically designed to disempower the Catholic Irish and every asset of their culture.

However, *Gaeilge*, and therefore the Irish identity, persevered secretly as a means of communication in rural areas and among the working class. The language was spoken, taught, and preserved in "hedge schools," outdoor gatherings that were mostly conducted at night to avoid punishments from British forces. Parents, teachers, and students risked everything to operate these hedge schools, usually conducted in cold, damp sheds, cabins, and cowhouses. So, the Irish people have been fighting to speak their native tongue for centuries.

Some of the Penal Laws were relaxed in 1782, following growing public discontent with religious restrictions. However, these measures fell far short of full Catholic Emancipation, which would not be achieved until 1829. Despite the easing of certain laws, the Irish language continued to decline, and many Catholic families still relied on hedge schools to educate their children outside the state system. In 1831, a state system of primary schools was rolled out nationally; however, English was still the primary language of education, and students were strongly discouraged from speaking *Gaeilge*. During this period, a tally stick, or *bata scóir*, was introduced in schools. With this practice, students wore a stick on a piece of string around their necks throughout the school day. Each time they spoke Irish, a notch would be carved into the stick, and these students would then be physically punished based on the number of notches received that day.

After six hundred years, roughly 50 percent of the country was still Irish speaking monolinguals, as per the 1841 census. However, by the 1851 census, the population in Ireland dropped by almost two million because of the Great Famine. In 1845, the disease blight struck Ireland's potato crop, devastating the people's primary food source. This resulted in roughly one million people emigrating, primarily to the United States, Britain, and Australia, and another roughly one million perished from hunger. The Great Famine affected the majority of people on the island, but especially devastated the poorest of the population, many of whom were Irish speakers. With this significant loss, the language faced seemingly irreparable damage.

Groups Supporting *Gaeilge*'s Revival

The Gaelic Revival, or *Athbheochan na Gaeilge*, of the late nineteenth century restored a sense of pride and passion in the Irish language throughout Ireland. By this point, the language had declined significantly as a spoken language but remained in rural areas, while English remained the official language of the island. To encourage use of the Irish language, the Society for the Preservation of the Irish Language formed in 1876. Their main focus was to "preserve the Irish Language in those parts of the country where it is spoken, with a view to its further extension and cultivation."

In 1893, the Gaelic League, or *Conradh na Gaeilge*, was founded to normalize the speaking of Irish in everyday life in an otherwise Anglicized nation. The founders of the organization, Eoin MacNeill and Douglas Hyde, felt that many contemporary Irish language groups were focused only on literature and the written language. The founders felt people should be connecting with the public and preserving the spoken word. *Conradh na Gaeilge* grew slowly in the beginning, but branches of the organization were established in Ireland, the Americas, England, and Scotland. By 1906, over nine hundred branches had been founded. The organization cultivated their own independent education system comprised of summer schools, language classes, and training courses for educators. They fought tirelessly for the Irish language to have a central role in all stages of the education system, ensuring that every child had the opportunity to learn and speak their native tongue.

The Gaelic Athletic Association, *An Cumann Lúthchleas Gael*, was founded in 1884 with the goal of creating a space in which traditional and Indigenous sports or pastimes were nurtured and revived. The GAA brought a new life and vibrancy to the traditional Gaelic games of Gaelic football, hurling, handball, rounders, and camogie—all of which are still played both around the country and around the world to this day.

In promoting uniquely Irish sports, the GAA cultivated and fostered a sense of national pride, which naturally encouraged interest in all things Irish (including the language). Many members of the GAA were also part of the Gaelic League. The two organizations worked together, creating a space for discourse, ideas, and schemes to nourish and grow between the two, ultimately benefiting both organizations and preserving all things Irish.

Irish Independence and *Gaeilge*

After centuries of British rule, Irish people longed for full independence. The Easter Rising of 1916 was the peoples' breaking point after many years of attempting peaceful resolutions. It was the Irish War of Independence of 1919–1921 that brought the question of Irish freedom to the forefront of the nation. The war was fought through ambushes, assassinations, and sabotage instead of large battles.

The British forces responded to these efforts with harsh measures, including the deployment of the feared Black and Tans. The Black and Tans were British veterans of World War I deployed in Ireland to quell rebellious behavior and thought.

Brutal toward civilians and militia, they were dubbed the Black and Tans because their uniforms were a combination of left-over World War I British khaki and Royal Irish Constabulary (the police force in Ireland at the time) uniforms.

Although the war created great suffering, a belief that Irish independence was inevitable was growing. Both sides eventually sought negotiations as the conflict became increasingly bitter and costly.

THE ANGLO-IRISH TREATY

In December 1921, Irish and British leaders signed the Anglo-Irish Treaty. This treaty granted most of Ireland the status of a self-governing dominion within the British Commonwealth, known as the Irish Free State. However, six counties in the north, with a Protestant or ethnically British majority at the time, remained part of the United Kingdom; this became known as Northern Ireland. Some accepted this split, while others radically opposed it, leading to the Irish Civil War of 1922–1923. Despite the division, the 1921 treaty marked a major shift in Ireland's history: The country now had its own government, army, and increasing control over its own affairs.

THE IRISH FREE STATE

On December 6, 1922, the Irish Free State officially came into being. It marked the first time in centuries that Irish people governed their own nation.

Although not yet a full republic, the Free State began building its own institutions, economy, and cultural life. Over time, the remaining ties to Britain were gradually severed, leading to the full Republic of Ireland in 1949. However, the six counties of the Anglo-Irish Treaty remained part of the United Kingdom.

The Free State period was also one of healing and rebuilding after years of civil conflict, unrest, and social dysfunction.

IMPACT ON THE IRISH LANGUAGE

The events from 1919 to 1922 reignited national pride, and with it came a renewed focus on the Irish language as a way to restore and cultivate a truly Irish identity. Within the new Free State government, Irish became the official language of the Republic, alongside English, and made it compulsory in schools. As per the Irish Constitution, Irish is the first official language of the island whereas English is recognized as a second official language. The government of Ireland, *Dáil Éireann*, initiated a now century-long program of bilingualism. Government departments used Irish names, streets and signs carried both languages, and much more. Irish was presented as a key symbol of national identity, a link to Ireland's ancient heritage, and a statement of independence from British rule.

Gaeilge's Present

Thanks to the resilience of the Irish and *Athbheochan na Gaeilge*, the Irish language survived and continues to be spoken on the island and elsewhere, but what is its status now? In the most recent Irish census conducted in 2022, 1,873,997 people claimed an ability to speak *some* Irish. However, 55 percent of people who claimed to speak the language reported that they could not speak it well.

Those who are members of the Irish-speaking population come from vastly different backgrounds and upbringings with the language. Native speakers hail primarily from *Gaeltacht* regions (the areas on the island where Irish is, or was until recently, the primary spoken language of the community). *Gaeltacht* areas can be found within Counties Donegal, Galway, Mayo, Cork, Kerry, Waterford, and Meath. *Gaeilge* is, at large, the first language of the people in these areas, and a native speaker is referred to as a *cainteoirí dúchais*. There are three spoken dialects within *Gaeilge*: *Canúint Chonnacht* (Connacht dialect), *Canúint na Mumhan* (Munster dialect), and *Canúint Uladh* (Ulster dialect).

Gaeilge in Schools

Béarla (English) has impacted the prosperity of the Irish language due to its accessibility and presence in media. Nowadays, Irish children who are being raised speaking only one language (*Gaeilge*) are surrounded by English speakers on TV, on the radio, in music, and socially.

However, for *Gaeltacht* areas to prosper, *Gaeilge* must be used at home, socially, and within the community. To value Irish-language teaching, all primary and secondary schools in any *Gaeltacht* area are regarded as *scoileanna Gaeltachta* (*Gaeltacht* schools), where *Gaeilge* being the sole language of instruction is a requirement, and a given.

School systems within Ireland will teach in English or in Irish (called English-medium or Irish-medium schools, respectively). Others are the *Gaeltacht* schools mentioned previously. Irish-medium primary schools are called *Gaelscoileanna* and are not located in a *Gaeltacht* area. There are almost two hundred *Gaelscoileanna* in Ireland with over forty thousand children being educated in Irish. Irish-medium secondary schools are called *Gaelcholáistí* and there are over twelve thousand students being educated in Irish at a secondary level across fifty schools. All *scoileanna Gaeltachta*, *Gaelscoileanna*, and *Gaelcholáistí* operate through speaking Irish exclusively.

With the establishment of the Irish Free State in 1922, *Gaeilge* received official status as the "national language" of the country and became a compulsory subject in *all* Irish schools. However, whether or not the Irish language education system is fit for purpose and adequately teaches the language to students is often debated and disputed. Many believe the curriculum focuses too much on literary analysis as opposed to basic, everyday conversational and communicative skills. The language has unfortunately acquired a negative connotation in many cases. When asked "Why can't you speak your own native language?" many Irish people will say that it's because of the way it's taught. Outside of the *Gaeltacht* areas, most can't view the language outside the curriculum or the four walls of a classroom. And, unfortunately, some Irish people do not engage with the language ever again after leaving school.

Worldwide Appreciation of the Irish Language

Despite the challenges, there's still hope in reviving the passion for the Irish language. The younger generation are breathing a new life into the language and seeking connection with their heritage and culture. Irish culture is a tale of resilience and combating colonialism, inspiring those outside of an Irish heritage.

To truly understand Ireland, you must understand the Irish language. Its names, traditions, idioms, place-names, music, dance, and literature are intertwined with the language, and to reconnect with a cultural identity, people are reconnecting with the language that shapes it. Regardless of educational policies or governmental initiatives, people are reclaiming the language that was stolen from them for centuries—a language that their ancestors were penalized and punished for speaking. Those who may have had a negative experience with the language in school are now taking it upon themselves to learn it independently, even a great number of years after leaving the education system. Expats are taking the language with them to every corner of the world with pride. People across the globe are learning the language to connect with their heritage and ancestors, or to simply show support to a repressed group who are still fighting tirelessly for their language all these centuries later.

Gaeilge in Media

For a language to be preserved, it needs to be seen, heard, and spoken daily, and the Irish-language media industry is certainly spearheading this ideology. *TG4* is Ireland's main Irish-language public service broadcaster and TV channel, and it was founded in 1996. On average, 1.2 million people in Ireland tune into the channel on a weekly basis. The channel runs a news service and broadcasts live sports, music shows, documentaries, and more. Programming specifically for children was an integral aspect of the channel since its founding in 1996, and in 2023, the *Cúla4* channel was launched. The channel airs Irish-language programs for kids up to twelve years old. None of the programs offer English subtitles in order to encourage Irish fluency.

In the village of Casla, *Raidió na Gaeltachta* is headquartered: Ireland's first Irish-language radio station. Founded in 1972, the station initially only broadcasted for two hours a day, and listeners could only tune in if they were near or in a *Gaeltacht* area. The station now has studios all over Ireland. The listenership of *Raidió na Gaeltachta* is likely mostly fluent

Irish speakers because the station caters toward the *Gaeltacht* population. There are three other Irish-language radio stations: *Raidió Rí-Rá* and *Raidió na Life* in Dublin, and *Raidió Fáilte* in Belfast.

Not only is *Gaeilge* taking over the airwaves and the TV screens of the nation, but it's also taking over the big screen. Irish-language films and filmmakers are paving a path for themselves and for the language toward Hollywood. For example, *An Cailín Ciúin* (The Quiet Girl) is an Irish-language drama film based on the 2010 novella *Foster* by Claire Keegan. The film is set in the year 1981 and follows the story of a young girl, raised by neglectful parents, who is sent to stay with distant relatives in the *Gaeltacht* area of *An Rinn*, County Waterford. *An Cailín Ciúin* initially premiered at the 72nd Berlin International Festival and won two awards, and it was then selected as Ireland's submission for Best International Feature Film at the 95th Academy Awards. The Irish language is preserved through traditional music and song styles; however, *Gaeilge* is also being used by artists as a modern medium of expression. There are very few, if any, forms of media and the arts in which the Irish language hasn't been incorporated.

Gaeilge Online

Fluent Irish speakers and learners alike have created spaces on social media platforms to connect and grow with the language. The hashtag #gaeilge continues to gain more traction daily with thousands engaging with the beautiful language. Irish teachers and scholars are creating accounts to share their knowledge with the masses, and audiences are flocking toward this content. People who struggled with the language in school are now reaching out to seek guidance and support to begin their independent learning journey. People who have never even heard of *Gaeilge* and weren't aware that the Irish language existed are now discovering it, learning about the history, and showing their support. With a simple click of a button, social media is giving people access to a language's history and a culture that has been preserved and nurtured for centuries.

Gaeilge's Future

Mar fhocal scoir (as a final word), is the future of the Irish language safe? Though things are looking up, there's no way to say for sure. There is still a lot of work to be done to preserve, promote, and support *Gaeltacht* areas. Some say the education system and curriculum are flawed and there is a serious lack of governmental funding in the Irish language sector. Though *Gaeilge* is trendy right now, people have fought for this language and its preservation for centuries. So, if you can incorporate at least one phrase or word *as Gaeilge* into your everyday interactions, social media posts, or emails, you're placing a brick in a stronger, unified future for the language and paying homage to the tireless work of those who came before.

2 A Note on Pronunciation

The phonetic system and pronunciations of the Irish language may be confusing at first. However, like any other language, there are patterns and sequences to decode the pronunciation of words *as Gaeilge*. Some people claim that "Irish names make no sense," or ask, "Why are there so many vowels so close together?!" and so on. When a celebrity with a name *as Gaeilge* appears in media outside Ireland, typically the first few minutes of the conversation will consist of the person defending the spelling and pronunciation of their name. The most important thing to remember from this point on is that Irish is not English, it does not look like English, and it should not and will not sound like English. Irish is a Celtic language, and English is a Germanic language. Therefore, they will naturally be extremely different on every and all grounds. So, this section will dive into how to read the words in this book and therefore, speak the language.

The Alphabet

First, anyone who wants to learn the language must learn the alphabet, called *Aibítir na Gaeilge*. Not all letters in the English alphabet are present in the Irish alphabet; you will not see the letters *j*, *k*, *q*, *v*, *w*, *x*, *y*, or *z* in any words *as Gaeilge*. Well, apart from in some loanwords like *zú* (zoo) and *vardrús* (wardrobe), and scientific terminology. The vowels (*a*, *e*, *i*, *o*, *u*) can be accented with an acute accent, which is referred to as a *síneadh fada*, literally translating to "a long stretch." When a *síneadh fada* is present on a vowel, the sound the vowel makes is stretched out, as the name suggests.

a	(ah)	á	(awww)
e	(eh)	é	(ayyyy)
i	(ih)	í	(eeeeee)
o	(uh)	ó	(ohhhh)
u	(uh)	ú	(oooooo)

Another important note about the vowels in Irish is that *a*, *o*, and *u* are considered broad vowels, and *e* and *i* are considered slender vowels. This is crucial to understanding the broad and slender consonants and how they're pronounced. The pronunciation of letters, such as *d*, *t*, *s*, and *r*, can vary depending on whether they're broad or slender. A consonant is broad if it is surrounded by broad vowels (*a*, *o*, *u*), and it's slender if surrounded by slender vowels (*i*, *e*).

Broad d	/d̪ˠ/	**Slender d**	/dʲ/
Broad t	/t̪ˠ/	**Slender t**	/tʲ/
Broad *s*	*(sssss)* /s/	**Slender *s***	*(shhh)* /ʃ/
Broad *r*	/ɹ/	**Slender *r***	/ɾʲ/ (rolled / tapped)

The broad *d* and *t* sound similar, and to pronounce these letters, the tongue is placed against the back of your top teeth; this will produce a slightly softer sound than the sound of the letters in English. The slender *d* sounds like an electric pulse or charge, and the slender *t* sounds like a droplet of water sizzling on a hot pan. The letter *s* is less complicated. The broad *s* is the *(ssss)* sound most are familiar with, like in "snake." And the slender *s* sound is *(shhh)*. When it comes to the letter *r*, the broad *r* is the same as in English, like a pirate's rrrrrrr. But the slender *r* is comparable to the single "*r* roll" sound heard in Spanish, when the tongue is flicked off the hard palate. If you're still following along, *maith thú* (go you!), but that's not all.

Special Letter Combinations

There are some special sounds that result from particular letter combinations, and you must be able to decode and pronounce these sounds *as Gaeilge*. Many of these occur when a *séimhiú* (lenition or "a softening") is applied to a letter. The *séimhiú* presents itself in written Irish as the letter *h* added after the first consonant of a word and can be applied to the following letters: *b, c, d, f, g, m, p, and s.*

When and why a *séimhiú* is applied would require a whole book in and of itself, so for now, just focus on how these letter combinations sound.

bh	*(v)* or *(w)*
ch	/ç/ (slender, like a cat's hiss) /x/ (broad, mid-gutteral)
*dh**	*(y)* or /j/y/ (from the back of the throat)
fh	silent
*gh**	/j/y/ (from the back of the throat)
mh	*(v)* or *(w)*
ph	*(f)*
th	*(h)*

*The sounding of the *dh* and *gh* combinations can be compared to the sound made in the back of the throat when gargling mouthwash.

Please note that the pronunciation of *Gaeilge* isn't an exact science, and there can be vast differences between the *canúintí*, or the spoken dialects. You must expose yourself to native and fluent speakers via the media to train your ear to these unique sounds, not just attempt to speak the language by comparing it to English.

3 Greetings, Farewells, and Conversations

This chapter is all about everyday, conversational Irish. In the following pages, you will find phrases to get you through the first few minutes of a conversation *as Gaeilge*. As the proverb says, *beatha teanga í a labhairt*, or “the life of a language is in its speaking.” So, choose to speak *Gaeilge* and keep the language alive by making some of these simple swaps. Whether your goal is to incorporate *Gaeilge* into your emails or social media posts, or you want to replace English day-to-day phrases with their *Gaeilge* counterparts, this chapter has it all.

a chara / a chairde NOUN

(ah KHAWR-rah) / (a KHAWR-jah)

my friend(s) / Dear Sir or Madam

A chara is the phrase used to formally address someone at the beginning of a letter, email, or text message, with the plural being ***a chairde***. This phrase is comparable to the "Dear Sir / Madam" you see in English, where the name of the recipient is not known to the sender, or if first-name basis has not yet been reached. However, ***a chara*** more literally translates to "O friend," meaning it can also be used in informal circumstances. The word *cara*, meaning "friend," is believed to derive from the Italian word *cara* meaning "beloved or dear." So, ***a chara*** is used frequently in conversational Irish to address a friend or close companion, as well as in formal circumstances like sending an email.

The Particle *A* **The particle *a* in *a chara* denotes the vocative case in the Irish language—the case used to address a person. In the vocative, the name or noun following the particle *a* can be modified. For example, *cara*, meaning "friend," but *a chara*. You see that sneaky letter *h* that's added in the vocative case? That's known as a *séimhiú* (i.e., a whole grammatical can of worms that is touched on in Chapter 2).**

a chroí / a stór NOUN

(ah khree) / (ah sthore)

my love; my darling; my beloved

If you feel like *a chara* just isn't cutting it, and you want to express further fondness for the person you're addressing, then the phrases ***a chroí*** and ***a stór*** are for you. Although these phrases translate to "my love," "my darling," or "my beloved," like many phrases in the Irish language, they're multifunctional. You can of course use these phrases to address a romantic partner or someone you bestow love for, but they can also be used in a platonic, warm manner. For example, close friends could address each other as ***a chroí***, grannies and granddads can address their little ones as ***a stór***, and so on. Taking a step further to look at literal translations and better understand the origin of these phrases, *croí* translates to "heart" and *stór* translates to "treasure." That's just adorable!

Making Things Cute An alternative form of ***a stór*** that is commonly used in the Irish language is *a stóirín (ah sthore-een)*. The suffix *-ín* is added to words to express a further sense of smallness or cuteness, similar to words like "puppy," "daddy," and "mommy" in English that end in a *y*. So, in this case, *a stóirín* translates to "my little darling," or "my little treasure."

a chuisle NOUN

(ah KHWISH-la)

my pulse

The word *cuisle* directly translates to "pulse," but it can be seen more commonly used in a declaration of love or as a term of endearment. There is no direct way to say "I love you" in the Irish language. Instead, phrases such as *a chuisle* are used to show your adoration and dedication to a romantic partner. Referring to someone as *a chuisle* infers that your love for them surges through your veins. Nothing screams burning passion more than telling someone that they are your pulse; the very reason your heart beats. Anatomical, yet romantic, it doesn't get much better than that. This sweet nothing, adapted from the longer declaration of love *a chuisle, mo chroí*, which translates to "the pulse of my heart," has been used as a term of endearment for centuries but gained further notoriety after the success of the early twentieth-century love song "Macushla," an anglicized spelling of the infamous phrase. Stemming from Middle Irish, the word *cuisle* not only refers to one's veins, but to narrow columns and streams in a broader sense. Therefore, depending on context or the word that immediately precedes or follows *cuisle*, the meaning can vastly change. For example, *ceol cuisle* refers to flute music, music produced by the blowing of air through a narrow passage.

An bhfuil tú ag coinneáil go maith? PHRASE

(on will thoo egg kwin-awl guh maah)

How are you? Are you keeping well?

An bhfuil tú ag coinneáil go maith? is a great alternative to the standard *Conas atá tú?* meaning "How are you?" This phrase could be used to greet someone that you haven't seen in a while, and you want to check in to see how they've been. ***An bhfuil tú ag coinneáil go maith?*** is an invitation for the recipient to fill you in on what's been going on in their life and really give you the rundown. For example, "I haven't seen you in forever! ***An bhfuil tú ag coinneáil go maith?***" A simple "How are you?" can be brushed off with a nonchalant "I'm grand" or "There's not a loss on me," which really divulge little to no information as to how the person is actually doing, and the conversation will move on. However, in asking someone "How are you keeping?" it opens the conversation up for a more broad, in-depth update. *Ag coinneáil* is the verbal noun, or the *-ing* format of the verb *coinnigh (kwin-yih)* meaning "to keep or maintain." Therefore, you can think of the phrase ***An bhfuil tú ag coinneáil go maith?*** as a means of conducting a maintenance check on those nearest and dearest to you.

An dtuigeann tú? PHRASE

(on DIG-in thoo)

Do you understand?

Perhaps you're familiar with the expression "Ya dig?," meaning "You catch my drift?" or "Do you follow my lead?," but did you know that the Irish language is to thank for this phrase? The way to say, "Do you understand?" *as Gaeilge* is ***An dtuigeann tú?***, with the *dtuigeann* being pronounced like "diggin." The "dig" in "Ya dig?" doesn't have any clear meaning, as if it referred to literal digging with a shovel; it's hard to form a correlation between that and the way in which the phrase is used. Therefore, it's commonly thought the "dig" in "Ya dig?" is a loanword from ***An dtuigeann tú?*** *as Gaeilge*.

This is a perfect example of Hiberno-English (the influence the Irish language has on the way in which English is spoken in Ireland and the phrases that are used). Like in the case of "Ya dig?," these phrases can often make no sense in English because they are formed around loanwords from *Gaeilge*. Many examples of Hiberno-English have traveled around the world with Irish people, have gained traction, and are largely understood by many. However, most Hiberno-English phrases and words are colloquial, predominantly used in Ireland, and often leave people confused because they don't make sense unless you understand where they come from: *Gaeilge*.

Aon chraic / scéal? PHRASE

(ayn chrack / sh-kayl)

What's up?

The word *craic* is one of the most versatile Irishisms. The Irish language borrows this word from the Old English word *cracian* meaning "a sharp noise or abrupt sound," which morphed into *crack* meaning "a general lively atmosphere." This English word was passed onto the Irish by means of the Scots in the mid-twentieth century where it took on a new, Gaelic form in the spelling *craic*. Today, *craic* has shape-shifted and adapted within Hiberno-English slang to be used in a many scenarios.

- ***"Aon chraic / scéal?"***
  What's up? Have you any stories / news / gossip for me?
- ***"We had mighty craic."***
  We had so much fun. / We had an amazing time.
- ***"The craic was ninety."***
  We had the best time (the *highest* attainable level of *craic*).
- ***"He's no craic at all."***
  He's not a good sport. / He's a sore loser.
- ***"Sure, you know the craic."***
  You know what's happening. / You understand the situation.
- ***"She's some craic."*** (sarcastically)
  She's no fun, she's boring.

Seldom a day goes by in Ireland that you don't encounter the word *craic* in one form or another.

ar bís ADJECTIVE

(air beesh)

excited

To be ***ar bís*** is a very specific kind of excitement. This expression encompasses an element of suspense, like being "on tenterhooks" (that you simply can't wait for what's about to happen). For that reason, it can be used to express that you are in a state of suspenseful and anticipatory excitement. For example, if asked, "Are you looking forward to the party later?" you could respond that you are ***ar bís!*** Also, you could describe yourself as being ***ar bís*** in the lead-up to a reunion with a friend who you've not seen in quite some time. An Irish-English equivalent to ***ar bís*** is "buzzing," which is used as such: "I'm buzzing to see you later!" To express that you are ***ar bís*** and use it in a sentence, one would say *tá mé ar bís (taw may air beesh)*, translating to "I am excited."

Pronouncing the Letter S The way in which the letter *s* is sounded in Irish is dependent on its closest vowels. Like many consonants *as Gaeilge*, this letter has a slender and a broad pronunciation variation. When the letter *s* is surrounded by slender vowels (*i*, *e*), it is pronounced *(shhh)*, like the name *Seán (shaun)*. When the letter *s* is surrounded by broad vowels (*a*, *o*, *u*), it is pronounced *(ssss)*, like the name *Saoirse (seer-shah)*.

ar buile ADJECTIVE

(air BWIL-ah)

mad; angry; furious

If you ever find yourself to be ***ar buile***, it's time to take a time-out. Equally, if someone around you describes themself as being ***ar buile***, it's time for some damage control. To be ***ar buile*** is to be furious, in a frenzy, infuriated, in a mad rage, or on a warpath. Not good. Using this expression in a sentence follows the same format as *ar bís*—one would say *tá mé ar buile*, literally translating to "I am furious."

Colors in the Irish language are used to depict emotions, and anger is no exception. Unsurprisingly, *dearg* (red) is the color used to depict anger. If one is *ar buile dhearg*, they are raging mad. An Irish-English colloquialism that stems from this phrase is "to be bulling," which means to be angry. For example, "I'm bulling I didn't get the job." One might assume that this comes from the noun "bull" and their tempered reputation, but the phrase's origin can be traced back to ***ar buile*** from *Gaeilge*.

The Puck Goat ***An Poc Ar Buile*, translating to "The Mad Puck Goat," is a traditional patriotic fight song (sung by the Irish group The Chieftains and others) and associated with the seventeenth-century festival called the Puck Fair. This is an annual fair held in Killorglin, County Kerry and is renowned for its tradition where a goat is crowned the Puck King and enthroned on a pedestal in the town square for three days.**

bail ó Dhia ort INTERJECTION

(ball oh yee-ah urt)

blessings of God on you; God love ya

Bail ó Dhia ort is an incredibly flexible phrase depending on the context in which it is used. *Bail* translating to "prosperity," *ó Dhia* meaning "from God," and the prepositional pronoun *ort* meaning "on you," come together harmoniously in this case to produce a phrase that Irish speakers couldn't live without. In its most integral form, ***bail ó Dhia ort*** serves to wish God's blessing upon a person. It is often used as a greeting or opening on TV and radio when addressing the audience, or at the beginning of a speech. Used as a sign of respect, this phrase bestows good wishes upon the crowd before you. ***Bail ó Dhia ort*** can also be used to sympathize or empathize with a person. For example, if a friend was to confide in you that they're under a lot of pressure at work, you could respond with ***bail ó Dhia ort*** to express your understanding of their situation. In this case, the phrase operates in a similar manner to the Irishisms "God love ya" and "ya poor thing." In other circumstances, ***bail ó Dhia ort*** is also used to praise or commend someone. For example, if someone was to share exciting news about a promotion at their job, you could respond with ***bail ó Dhia ort***, comparable to the Irishism "good on ya," meaning good for you.

beidh le feiceáil PHRASE

(bye leh feck-awl)

we shall see; time will tell

When times are uncertain and you're not sure what lies ahead of you, ***beidh le feiceáil*** is the perfect phrase to fill a gap or wrap up a conversation. *Le feiceáil* directly translated is "to be seen," with *beidh* being the future tense conjugation of the verb *bí*, "to be." Therefore, this phrase literally translates to "will be seen." However, it is used more in the sense of "we shall see" or "time will tell." For example, "Do you know how many people are coming to the party?" "***Beidh le feiceáil.***"

The verb *feic* is often a cause for chuckles among school students in Ireland when learning *Gaeilge*. In the Irish language, it means "to see"; however, this word has many vernacular meanings in Hiberno-English. The anglicized spelling "feck" is used in Ireland as an alternative to the four-letter *f*-word profanity. "Feck" is not as harsh as that *other* word and is used to express disbelief, anger, pain, or surprise. Many young people in Ireland are aware of the word "feck" and its connotations, which yields lots of giggles in the classroom when learning about the verb *feic* (to see) in the Irish language.

Beidh mé ag caint leat ar ball PHRASE

(bye may egg cye-nch lyath air ball)

I'll chat to you later

Beidh mé ag caint leat ar ball is a fabulous phrase to use when parting ways with someone and ending a conversation. It's not as formal and definitive as a "goodbye," but instead, "I'll chat with you later." When broken down, the literal translation leaves little room for confusion (kind of). *Beidh mé* "I will be," *ag caint leat* "chatting with you," and *ar ball* "later," or "earlier," depending on the context. *Ar ball* can mean "earlier on," "a while ago," or "later." This can be confusing, but you can rely on context and verb tenses for clarity. For example, "I cleaned my room *ar ball*" versus "I will clean my room *ar ball*."

The Irish Goodbye The notion of "the Irish Goodbye" has been popularized in recent media and pop culture. It is depicted as being a quick, smooth, undetectable exit from an event or a social gathering without *actually* saying goodbye to anyone. However, a true Irish Goodbye can often take hours with multiple attempts to leave being made, ultimately ending in a long series of "bye bye, bye now, alrighty, bye bye now, thanks a mil, chat to you soon, alright mind yourself, byeeeeeee bye bye." An Irish Goodbye is *anything* but quick, smooth, or undetectable.

beir bua NOUN

(behr boo-ah)

best wishes

There is an undeniable trend being seen both in Ireland and across the pond whereby people are making efforts to incorporate as much *Gaeilge* into their everyday lives as possible, and emails are no exception. ***Beir bua*** is one of many options that you can use to sign off an email. Once again, this phrase is an example of when the literal translation and the context in which the phrase is used are quite different. The Irish verb *beir* means "to grab onto, to bear, to give birth to," stemming from the Old English word "beran," meaning "to bring forth." This sentiment has carried forward into modern-day *Gaeilge*, meaning that the verb *beir* really encapsulates a tight grasp, almost like a fistful. The noun *bua* means "triumph" or "victory." Therefore, when signing off an email with the phrase ***beir bua***, you are wishing upon the recipient that they go forth from that point on and bear victory and triumph. See, the literal translation is better than "best wishes." If you happen to be sending a strongly worded email or you don't wish triumph and victory on the recipient, ***beir bua*** might not be the best option for a sign-off, but don't worry, this chapter has you covered with other *neutral* email sign-offs as well.

b'fhéidir ADVERB

(bay-jur)

maybe; perhaps

As a simple conversation filler, ***b'fhéidir*** is a really easy word to throw in to add that *Gaeilge* flair to your speech. For example, "Are you going out tonight?" "***B'fhéidir***." (Extra marks for dragging out the word and pairing it with a cheeky wink to add some deviousness.)

The word *féidir* by itself can mean "possible," but it rarely stands on its own. In the case of ***b'fhéidir***, the word *ba* would be added before the *féidir* to signify the conditional tense. *Ba* (would) + *féidir* (possible) = "would be possible," "maybe," or "perhaps." In the Irish language, the letter *f* can act like a vowel in certain circumstances. As a general rule of thumb, an unstressed vowel at the end of one word followed by another unstressed vowel at the beginning of the next word are blended together. Therefore, *ba* is shortened to *b* to avoid the combination of two vowels, leaving the phrase ***b'fhéidir***. Problem solved.

Slender *R* and *D* Sounds This word is commonly used by Irish language educators as a means for learners to practice those tricky slender *r* and slender *d* sounds. As you can see, the letter *d* in ***b'fhéidir*** is surrounded by the slender vowel *i*, making it a slender *d*, and the letter *r* at the end of the word is surrounded by the slender vowel *i*, once again, making it a slender *r*.

buíochas le Dia INTERJECTION

(BWEE-kus leh JEE-ah)

thankfully; thanks be to God; thank goodness

Ah, the good old ***buíochas le Dia***. What Irish speaker's tool kit would be complete without it? Directly translating to "thanks with God," this phrase can also be used in a more general sense to express the sentiment of "thankfully." For example, "We made our flight just in time, ***buíochas le Dia***," or "It has finally stopped raining, ***buíochas le Dia***!" The word *buíochas*, meaning "gratitude," stems from the Old Irish word *buidech*, meaning "well-disposed" or "grateful." *Le* is the preposition "with," and *Dia* means "God," which will continue to be seen in further phrases. To add further emphasis to this phrase, the adjective *mór* meaning "big" can be added, resulting in *buíochas mór le Dia*, literally meaning "big thanks to God."

"Thanks be to God" is an extremely common idiom preserved by older generations in Ireland; however, phrases as such are well engrained in the minds and vernacular of the youth also. If you wish to not express gratitude to God in particular, this phrase can be easily adapted to best suit the circumstances. Simply replace *Dia* with the name of the person you wish to thank. For example, *buíochas le Máire* (thanks to Mary), *buíochas le Pádraig* (thanks to Patrick), or *buíochas le Ruairí* (thanks to Rory).

céad míle fáilte PHRASE

(kayd MEE-lah FAWL-cha)

welcome; a hundred thousand welcomes

Where would the isle of Ireland be without the infamous ***céad míle fáilte***? This greeting has become synonymous with the idea of warm Irish hospitality and the nation's welcoming nature. Literally translating to "a hundred thousand welcomes"—*céad* (one hundred), *míle* (one thousand), *fáilte* (welcomes)—this phrase can be seen etched and printed on signage above shops, bars, hotels, and houses all around the country. The earliest known use of this phrase dates to the early 1800s in the writings of Sydney Morgan, an Irish novelist. The Irish people are known for having a very open mindset when it comes to welcoming people into their homes or businesses and there has traditionally been a strong sense of community within localities. This stems back to the ancient traditions of *bothántaíocht* and *seanchas* that will be discussed further in Chapter 4: Fun and Entertainment. So, if you were to rock up to a rural Irish pub in need of assistance or directions, the locals would spring into action and there would be no shortage of people ready and willing to help you. These selfless characteristics reflect the good nature of the Irish people; a trait both recognized and adored by many.

ceart go leor / maith go leor ADJECTIVE

(kyart guh lyore) / (maah guh lyore)

okay

Ceart go leor and ***maith go leor*** are essential conversation fillers and responses to be aware of if you intend to engage in a conversation *as Gaeilge*. Figuratively translated, they mean "okay," but there's a further literal translation. *Ceart* means "correct," and *go leor* means "enough," therefore translating to "correct enough." Similarly, *maith* means "good," so therefore ***maith go leor*** means "good enough." Both these phrases can be used in agreement to a statement. For example, *Rachaimid go dtí an siopa anois* (We'll go to the shop now), with the appropriate response being ***ceart go leor*** or ***maith go leor***. Both these phrases can also be used as an adjective. An example of this is being asked *Conas mar a bhí an cheolchoirm?* (How was the concert?), and using ***ceart go leor*** or ***maith go leor*** as a response to describe the concert. If a person was to use either of these phrases in response to the question *Conas atá tú?* (How are you?), it would be an indication that maybe they're not doing *amazingly*. ***Ceart go leor*** and ***maith go leor*** don't have inherently negative or positive connotations, but there are various adjectives that could be used to infer a more positive or negative state of being. So, these phrases lie somewhere in the middle in no-man's-land but are perfectly acceptable to use as a term of agreeableness.

coinnigh ort PHRASE

(KWIN-yih urt)

keep it up; keep going

This expression is often heard at Gaelic games and sports matches and is typically paired with fiery encouragement. Coaches, parents, and supporters will be heard on the sidelines instructing the players to ***coinnigh ort***, meaning "keep it up" or "keep it going." ***Coinnigh ort*** is a combination of the verb *coinnigh*, translating to "keep" or "continue," and *ort*, which is the preposition pronoun "on you." Therefore, the expression can also bear the sentiment of "carry on" or "don't give up."

Off the football pitch, ***coinnigh ort*** can be used as words of encouragement for someone who may need a bit of a pick-me-up. Whether you're nearing the finish line or reaching the summit, a heartfelt or passionate ***coinnigh ort*** might just be what you need to go the extra mile.

Keep Her Lit The most comparable expression in colloquial English-Irish to ***coinnigh ort*** is "keep her lit." This expression bares the same meaning of "keep going" or "keep it up" and stems from the sentiment of keeping something "alight." The origins of this phrase can also be traced back to a story of an IRA (Irish Republican Army) ambush on British forces. An IRA volunteer instructed a fellow volunteer to "keep her lit," meaning to keep firing.

Conas atá tú? PHRASE

(CUH-nis a-THAW thoo)

How are you?

You won't get too far into a conversation *as Gaeilge* without asking someone **Conas atá tú?** *Conas* means "how," *atá* means "is," and *tú* means "you." This is the phrase used to ask someone "How are you?" as per standardized Irish; however, there are variations depending on the spoken dialects of Irish.

In *Gaeilge Chonnacht* (Connacht Irish), one would say *Cén chaoi 'bhfuil tú (cane kwee will thoo)*, directly translating to "What way is it that you are?" In *Gaeilge na Mumhan* (Munster Irish), one would ask *Conas 'tánn tú?* or *Conas atá agat?* These variations are most similar to standardized Irish. Finally, in *Gaeilge Uladh* (Ulster Irish), one would ask *Caidé mar atá tú? (cah-jay mar a-tah thoo)*. Each of these phrases is used when catching up with an old friend and, although informal, they are all considered polite to use when greeting someone you've just met. If greeting more than one person, all the standardized and dialectal variations just described are easily adaptable into the plural by simply swapping the *tú* for a *sibh (shiv)*. "*Conas atá sibh?*," "*Cén chaoi 'bhfuil sibh?*," "*Conas 'tánn sibh?*," or "*Caidé mar atá sibh?*" meaning "How are ye (you, plural)?"

creid é nó ná creid PHRASE

(crej ay no naw crej)

believe it or not

Throwing in a ***creid é nó ná creid*** is a great way to punctuate or pace a story, and it's a bonus that this phrase rolls off the tongue quite easily. Imagine the scenario: you're invested in depicting an event that occurred, and, right as you reach the climax of the story, you throw in a ***creid é nó ná creid*** (followed by a dramatic pause) to add suspense before wowing your audience with the big finale. Now, in retrospect, using the phrase ***creid é nó ná creid*** is not typically such a theatrical affair, but it is now in your arsenal to use with as much dramatic flair as you see fit. This expression fits well in the middle of a sentence to tee up the punchline, but it also works well at the start of a sentence to get straight to the point and preempt that you're about to blow some minds with a juicy piece of information.

Pronouncing *I's* and *D's* Using this phrase is the perfect opportunity to practice some crispy slender *d's* as you see at the end of the word *creid*. Given that there's a slender vowel, *i*, the letter *d* that follows is subsequently slender. If your audience isn't already in a trance from the amount of suspense you've built up by using this phrase, make sure you wow them with a display of impeccable pronunciation.

Deas bualadh leat PHRASE

(jahs BOO-lah lyath)

Nice to meet you

When you've just met someone, the phrase ***Deas bualadh leat*** is the most fitting way to wrap up the conversation and bid your *adieus*, as opposed to a general *slán* (goodbye). The literal translation of this phrase leaves little to the imagination, with *deas* translating to "nice," *bualadh* being the verb "to meet," and *leat* being the preposition "with you." However, the verb *bualadh* has an alternate meaning depending on the prepositions used alongside it. *Bualadh* followed by the preposition *le*, meaning "with," means "to meet somebody." On the other hand, *bualadh* can be followed by a pronoun that changes the meaning to "to hit or strike" somebody. For example, *bhuail mé le Seán* (I met Seán) versus *bhuail mé Seán* (I hit Seán). Accuracy and knowledge of prepositions play a huge role in the Irish language, and this is a perfect example. Another widely used version of this phrase is *Deas casadh leat (jahs caw-sah lyath)*, although this phrase would be most commonly heard and used in *Canúint Chonnacht* (Connacht dialect) or in the *Gaeltacht* areas of Connemara.

Bualadh Bos **The phrase used in Irish for "a round of applause" is *bualadh bos*. As just discussed, the verb *bualadh* can mean "to hit, strike, or bang" and the word *bos* on its own refers to the palm of the hand. Therefore, a round of applause *as Gaeilge* literally translates to "banging of the palms."**

Dia duit | Dia 's Muire duit INTERJECTION

(JEE-ah gwitch) | (JEE-ah ihs MWUR-ah gwitch)

hello | hello (response)

Perhaps one of the most important greetings, this entry will finally teach you how to say a simple "hello." In order to say hello *as Gaeilge*, there's another reference to *Dia* "God," which is followed by the prepositional pronoun *duit*, meaning "for you" or "to you." Therefore, when saying hello to someone *as Gaeilge*, you are essentially wishing God upon them or before them. ***Dia duit*** stems from the longer phrase *go mbeannaí Dia duit*, meaning "may God bless you." The mention of God appears in many greetings in various languages, for example, *adieu* and *adios* in French and Spanish, respectively, meaning "unto God." The word "goodbye" itself also originates from a contraction of the phrase "God be with ye."

The response to ***Dia duit*** is ***Dia 's Muire duit***, meaning "God and Mary to you," but it can even go further. Although not commonly used by Irish speakers, the phrase can be extended to *Dia 's Muire 's Pádraig duit*, meaning "God and Mary and (Saint) Patrick to you." Now, add another patron saint into the blessing with *Dia 's Muire 's Pádraig 's Bríd duit*, meaning "God and Mary and (Saint) Patrick and (Saint) Bridget to you." While it may not be commonly used by Irish speakers, it's a fun nugget of information or even a party piece to impress the *Gaeilgeoirí* (Irish speakers) in your life.

éasca péasca ADJECTIVE

(AYS-kah PAYS-kah)

easy peasy

This is a cute little expression that you can throw into your conversations to incorporate some *Gaeilge* in a fun way. Perhaps you've used the phrase "easy peasy lemon squeezy" at some point in your life, but now, you can use ***éasca péasca*** instead. The phrase ***éasca péasca*** came to life within the Irish language by means of mirroring the English phrase "easy peasy" and although usually Irish speakers don't support *Gaeilge* existing in the shadow of *Béarla*, this is a one-time exception. *Éasca* does indeed translate to "easy," while *péasca* has no inherent meaning individually other than in the context of this phrase, in the same way that "peasy" doesn't have any meaning in English.

Béarlachas **This phrase is an example of what is referred to among the Irish-speaking community as *Béarlachas*, meaning *Gaeilge* influenced by *Béarla* (English). There are many instances in which *Béarlachas* can damage the integrity of the Irish language and compromise grammatical accuracy; however, cases like this in which the language is mirroring English in a harmless, playful manner, are acceptable because *éasca péasca* is just too fun not to be sprinkled into your conversations.**

fadhb ar bith PHRASE

(fibe air bih)

no problem

Here is a fabulous example of a multifunctional expression. ***Fadhb ar bith*** can be used as a response in a wide variety of circumstances, most notably as an alternative to *tá fáilte romhat*, meaning "you're welcome." When used in an interaction in this context, it'll look like this: "*Go raibh maith agat as sin!*" (thanks for that), with the response being "***Fadhb ar bith***" (no problem). When used as an alternative to "you're welcome," this expression basically implies that it was no trouble at all. ***Fadhb ar bith*** can also be used as a general response to any statement that you're not opposed to. For example, if someone was to tell you that "*Táimid ag dul go dtí an siopa anois*" (We're going to the shop now), ***fadhb ar bith*** would be a perfectly adequate response if you're in favor of going. *Ar bith* can mean both "any" or "no," depending on the context, which can get confusing when referring to anywhere, nowhere, anybody, and nobody. For example: *An raibh duine ar bith ag an gcóisir?* (Was there anybody at the party?) versus *Ní raibh duine ar bith ag an gcóisir* (There was nobody at the party). If you were to isolate *ar bith*, there's really no way to decipher if it means "any" or "no," and that's why when it comes to *Gaeilge*, context is your best friend.

fan go gcloisfidh tú PHRASE

(fawn guh glish-ee thoo)

wait 'til you hear; I've got news for you

The Irish countryside, rural towns, and villages can be known for having quite a severe case of "small-town mindset," meaning they love a bit of gossip. Therefore, ***fan go gcloisfidh tú*** is a great phrase to whip out when you have a juicy piece of information to divulge. There's nothing to hide in this translation, with *fan* being the verb "to wait," *go* meaning "until," *gcloisfidh* being the future tense conjugation of the verb *clois* "to hear," and finally, the pronoun *tú*, meaning "you." The Irish people have an infatuation with news, stories, and gossip—when a new nugget of information has been acquired, this is the perfect phrase to build anticipation before sharing the tale. For example, "I was chatting to Máire after work and ***fan go gcloisfidh tú***." If someone were to say this, you'd know that the information they're about to share is going to be nothing other than scandalous. Similarly, this phrase could also be used as a great response to the question *Aon chraic / scéal?* (Any news / story?). If you answer that question with a ***fan go gcloisfidh tú***, the person you're chatting with is certainly in for a treat.

fútsa atá sé PHRASE

(FOOTS-a a-thaw shay)

it's up to you

If you regularly face decision paralysis, the expression ***fútsa atá sé*** is here to save the day. (By the way, if you didn't pick up on the rhyme in that first sentence, you're pronouncing *sé* wrong.) Figuratively translated, it means "it's up to you" or "you decide," but literally translated, it means "beneath you it is." This expression is most used in response to a question, for example: "What time should we leave at?" with the response "***Fútsa atá sé***" (It's up to you / I don't mind, you decide). The phrase can also be used at the end of a sentence to invite the other person to chime in with their opinion. So, if you want to pawn off the responsibility of choosing a movie to watch or picking a restaurant to eat at, simply use the expression ***fútsa atá sé*** to return the decision back to sender.

The Emphatic Suffix It's time to get excited about some grammar. The emphatic suffix refers to the unit *-sa (sah)* to emphasis ownership or possession. In English, the emphasis is expressed by verbally stressing the relevant word. For example, note the difference between "Do you care?" and "Do YOU care?" versus *An cuma leat?* and *An cuma leatsa?* In this case, the emphatic suffix *-sa* has been added to the prepositional pronoun *leat*, meaning "you."

gabh mo leithscéal INTERJECTION

(gaw muh leh-SHKAYL)

excuse me

The phrase used to say "excuse me" *as Gaeilge* is ***gabh mo leithscéal***, which literally translates to "take my excuse." (You're not really giving the other person much of a choice there, eh?) *Gabh* is the verb "to take" and stems from the Old Irish word *gaibid*, which means "to grasp or receive." *Mo* is the possessive adjective "my," and *leithscéal* is "excuse." If you look at the word *leithscéal* under a microscope, you'll see there's more to uncover than what meets the eye. *Scéal* is the Irish word for "story" and the *leith* you see preceding *scéal* in *leithscéal* stems from the word *leath*, meaning "half." So, the word *leithscéal* literally translates to "a half story," meaning you're getting not the full story or explanation but an excuse. If you're starting to think this sounds familiar and an awful lot like the expression "to tell a half-truth," you're on the right track. The etymology of the word *leithscéal* dates back to the period of Middle Irish from C.E. 900 to 1200, and the expression "to tell a half-truth" is recorded in use from 1628 onward. Therefore, it is feasible that the expression "to tell a half-truth" (to deceive someone, not tell them the full story, give an excuse) grew from the same concept behind the word *leithscéal*.

gan dabht / gan amhras ADVERB

(gawn doubt) / (gawn ow-ris)

without a doubt; undoubtedly

Gan dabht or ***gan amhras*** is a simple swap that can be used in a variety of circumstances as both a response and as a conversation filler. Literally and figuratively translating to "without doubt," the opportunities are endless with this phrase. For example, "Will I see you at the event later?" with the response being "***gan dabht***" or "***gan amhras***," meaning "undoubtedly, you will see me there." In this case, the phrase operates as a positive response to the question. ***Gan dabht / amhras*** can also be used as an affirmative response in agreement to something the other party has proposed. For example, "We're gonna need more paper plates for the party," with an appropriate response being "***gan dabht***" or "***gan amhras***," meaning that yes, without a doubt, more paper plates are needed. If you're thinking that the Irish word *dabht* bears a striking resemblance to the English word "doubt," you would be correct. Unfortunately, there is no interesting etymological explanation that both words stem from Latin or Old Irish; *dabht* is simply a borrowed word *as Gaeilge* from English. Therefore, if you want to avoid the *Béarlachas* and opt for a more innately Irish option, ***gan amhras*** is the phrase for you.

go dté (tú / sibh) slán PHRASE

(guh jay thoo / shiv slawn)

safe travels; go in good health

Go dté tú slán is a beautiful phrase to use when parting ways with someone you won't see for quite a while, or someone who is embarking on a significant journey. In wishing someone ***go dté tú slán***, you are wishing them "safe travels," or in a more literal sense, "may you go safe." The word *slán* itself means "safe" or "sound," and it is the word used *as Gaeilge* to say "goodbye" to someone. In the context of ***go dté tú slán***, the *slán* is not referring to "goodbye," but instead to the sentiment of safety. This phrase can be used to wish someone well as they embark on a physical journey, such as going traveling, but also in a figurative sense to those who may be embarking on a new path or journey in life. To address more than one person, ***go dté sibh slán*** can be used.

May the Road Not Rise to Meet You A common Irish blessing is "may the road rise to meet you"; however, this phrase is believed to originate from a mistranslation. It derives from the Irish phrase *go n-éirí an bóthar leat*. The verb *éirigh* in the Irish language bears many meanings, one of them being "to rise," but when paired with the preposition *le* (root of *leat*), it means "to succeed." Therefore, *go n-éirí an bóthar leat* would actually translate to "may you succeed along the road," or in a figurative sense, "may you succeed on the journey of life."

go mbeirimid beo ar an am seo arís PHRASE

(guh MERR-y-mwij by-oh air on awm shuh ah-reesh)

may we be alive this time next year

This is the perfect phrase to have in your back pocket, ready to whip out at big occasions such as birthdays, Christmas, or yearly group get-togethers. This phrase is used as a toast when surrounded by those dear to you, and although it harbors a slightly downcast sentiment, it usually creates a heartfelt and wholesome moment. The phrase literally translates to "may we be alive this time next year," implying that next Christmas or at the next birthday party in a year's time, no one will have kicked the bucket, and the same group of people will be coming together to make the same toast (hence the dark undertone). As a nation, the Irish people have a reputation of not shying away from death and they talk about the topic quite openly, so a phrase like this wouldn't be considered morbid, but instead a celebration. To make a toast to those you care about, wishing good health upon them so that you may all be alive and together once again twelve months down the line is equally special and poignant. This phrase bears an uncanny likeness to the more general Irish toast *sláinte*, which literally translates to "health" and means "cheers."

go n-éirí leat INTERJECTION

(guh neye-ree lyat)

good luck

You would use the phrase ***go n-éirí leat*** to wish someone good luck *as Gaeilge*. However, the literal translation of the phrase is "may you succeed." *Go n-éirí* bears the meaning "will / may succeed" and *leat* is the prepositional pronoun "with you," expressing upon whom you wish the success. If you want to wish success upon multiple people, simply swap the *leat* for the plural *libh (liv)*. *Go n-éirí* stems from the verb *éirigh*, a verb that holds a high status among the Irish-speaking community due to its versatility. The meaning of this verb changes drastically depending on the prepositions it is followed by. In this case, when *éirigh* is followed by the preposition *le* (with), it means "to succeed." When followed by the preposition *as* (out), it means "to retire" or to stop doing something. *Éirigh* also means "to rise," such as to get out of bed.

go raibh maith agat | go raibh míle maith agat INTERJECTION

(guh ruh mawh aw-guth) | (guh ruh MEE-lah mawh aw-guth)

thank you; may you have goodness

The true meaning of ***go raibh maith agat*** is so much more than just a boring "thank you." The *go raibh* in the phrase relates to the grammatical case used to wish something upon someone, like how the word "may" in English is used. *Maith* simply translates to "good" or "goodness," and *agat* is the prepositional pronoun "at you." Therefore, when responding ***go raibh maith agat*** to someone, you are wishing goodness upon them. How sweet. If you are extremely thankful to someone, this phrase can be extended to ***go raibh míle maith agat***, meaning "may a thousand goodnesses be upon you."

The word for "one thousand," *míle*, is a false cognate, and is often confused for "one million" due the spellings being so alike, so be careful. This false cognate appears in many other languages, such as *mille* in Italian, *mila* in Basque, and *mil* in Spanish. It is believed that this example of a false cognate in the Irish language is what gives life to the Hiberno-English idiom "thanks a mil," which is often lengthened to "thanks a million." However, if right were right, the phrase would actually be "thanks a thousand," shortened to "thanks a thous"? To be fair, "thanks a mil" rolls off the tongue a lot more smoothly. In an effort to rebuke this mistranslation, you could make "thanks a thousand" a thing and pay homage to the gorgeous Irish phrase ***go raibh míle maith agat***.

go tobann ADVERB

(guh THUB-inn)

suddenly

Among the Irish-speaking community, the phrase ***go tobann*** holds an almost meme-able reputation and is often used in a sarcastic tone by younger Irish speakers. Although the phrase simply translates to "suddenly" on the surface, the cultural significance goes much deeper. This phrase is overused in state exams for Irish teenagers at the end of secondary school, called the Leaving Certificate (or "the Leaving Cert"). For those taking Irish as a subject for the Leaving Cert, they will have to complete an Irish oral exam. One of the components of this exam is describing a series of events depicted by a series of six pictures. Typically, some kind of unexpected event will occur in this series of pictures. For example, a car crash, an accident, or a robbery. Therefore, the phrase ***go tobann*** is overused by students and teachers alike to build suspense in their narration before the climax of the story.

Normal People The Leaving Cert exams gained global notoriety as a result of the TV series *Normal People* starring Daisy Edgar-Jones and Paul Mescal. The show enamored millions worldwide with its insight into the life of a young adult in Ireland. Seeing the likes of Kourtney Kardashian posting about the debs (the Irish equivalent of prom) on her Instagram story was a pinch-me moment for many. What was once a niche, Irish coming-of-age experience was now being portrayed to a global audience.

grá | grá mór NOUN

(graw) | (graw more)

love

The Irish people share a strong connection to the word ***grá*** for many reasons. The word simply and directly translates to "love," but it carries a much deeper cultural and linguistic significance—it can be described as the heartbeat of the country. ***Grá*** is not just a word or phrase, and simply translating it to "love" doesn't do it justice. The word means love, passion, strength, vulnerability, heartbreak, and connection. Given that there is no direct way to say "I love you" in Irish, there are various declarations of love in the Irish language in which ***grá*** features. For example, *mo ghrá thú (muh ghraw hoo)*, meaning "you are my love" and *táim i ngrá leat (taw-im ih nraw lyat)*, meaning "I am in love with you." The phrase ***grá mór***, meaning "big love" or "lots of love," has gained popularity and filtered into Irish culture. ***Grá mór*** is littered across social media and also on clothes, tattoos, and art.

Although ***grá*** is a word filled with passion, it doesn't always have to refer to a romantic or affectionate love. In a more casual sense, the word is used to describe having a particular fondness, longing, or craving for something. For example, "I have an awful ***grá*** on me for a pint after work." ("Awful" is used as a positive adjective as well as a negative in Irish slang, similar to "immense.")

gurab amhlaidh duit INTERJECTION

(GUH-rub OW-lee gwitch)

likewise; same to you

This phrase roughly translates to "likewise" or "same to you" and functions as a "return to sender" or "Uno reverse" action. This is the perfect response to use if someone is wishing you a Merry Christmas, Happy New Year, Happy St. Patrick's Day, Happy Easter, or in general wishing good luck upon you. Using this phrase avoids a clunky repetition of the same phrase back to the kind person and results in a much smoother flow to the conversation. For example, if someone was to wish you *Nollaig Shona duit (nuh-lig hun-ah gwitch)*, meaning "Happy Christmas to you," the appropriate response would be ***gurab amhlaidh duit!***, of course, meaning "likewise" or "same to you." If more than one person has wished you a Happy Christmas, the prepositional pronoun *duit* meaning "to you" can be swapped for the plural *daoibh*, meaning "to ye." Make sure you don't get caught out using this phrase as a response to a waiter when they tell you to enjoy your meal—your quick "you too!" will be followed by an awkward blank stare.

Happy Christmas or Merry Christmas . . . ? You'll rarely hear an Irish person wishing someone a "Merry Christmas." The expression *Nollaig Shona duit* is used to wish someone a "Merry Christmas" *as Gaeilge* and translates to "A happy Christmas to you." The word *sona* in Irish means "happy," which was adapted in English, making this difference of expressions a perfect example of Hiberno-English.

haigh / haileo INTERJECTION

(hi) / (hello)

hi / hello

For those who might want an alternative way to say "hello" *as Gaeilge* that doesn't bring *Dia* (God) into the equation, this one's for you. ***Haigh*** and ***haileo*** are simply just Gaelicized spellings of the words "hi" and "hello" and are pronounced in the exact same way. Now, do these words fundamentally go against the principle of avoiding *Béarlachas*? Yes. Therefore, many *Gaeilge* enthusiasts and purists would completely blacklist these variations. Although *Gaeilge* is an ancient language with a rich history and deep roots in mythology and religion, the language is being modernized by a new generation of Irish speakers. Therefore, the language is adapting to fit changing linguistic and communicative needs. Of course, when speaking Irish, if you were to say ***haigh*** or ***haileo***, no one is to know whether you used these modern Gaelicized spellings or if you've fallen back onto *Béarla*. However, ***haigh*** and ***haileo*** will commonly be seen used in informal emails and text messages. Now, it's hard to avoid mentions of God/religion completely when speaking Irish, as *Dia* (meaning "God") crops up in many of the blessings used in everyday greetings, but remember that many languages do this.

i ndáiríre? | dáiríre píre INTERJECTION

(ih naw-ree-rah?) | (daw-ree-rah pee-rah)

Seriously? / Really? | Seriously / Really

This fun phrase is used to express disbelief in the same sentiment as "REALLY?!," "REALLY, REALLY!" or similarly, "SERIOUSLY?!," "SERIOUSLY!" Of course, the level of excitement or disbelief depends on the tone and delivery, but ultimately this flexible phrase can be used in a variety of scenarios. ***I ndáiríre?***, meaning "really / seriously?" is the question, with ***dáiríre píre*** being the response. For example, if your friend was to tell you that they bought a house, you could respond with "***I ndáiríre?!***," prompting the subsequent response "***Dáiríre píre!***" from them. However, this phrase can also be used with a sly tone to express disappointed disbelief. So, if a friend told you they did something bad, you could respond with a disapproving ***i ndáiríre?*** and a furrowed brow. The alliteration from the slender *r*'s gives this phrase a fun, sharp sound that adds suspense to any conversation.

Practice Your *R*'s ***I ndáiríre? Dáiríre píre*** is the perfect opportunity to practice your pronunciation of the slender *r* in Irish as they are littered all over. The slender *r* sound is most prevalent in the Connacht or Connemara dialect of Irish, meaning that native speakers from this region are the experts of this unique sound that many learners struggle with. Focus on stiffening the tongue and flicking it off the palate of the mouth or back of the teeth to produce a single *r* roll.

is dócha INTERJECTION

(iss doe-khah)

I suppose so; probably

Is dócha is another example of the many multifunctional phrases in the Irish language, making it a valuable tool for all those intending to throw *cúpla focal* (a few words) into their daily interactions. This phrase can be translated in a few similar ways and is most commonly used in the context of "I suppose so" or "probably." ***Is dócha*** can function independently as an answer or a statement, or it can also be used in a sentence. For example, if someone was to ask you "*An mbeidh sé báisteach amárach meastú?*" (Will it be rainy tomorrow do you think?), an appropriate response would be "*Beidh, is dócha,*" meaning "It will, probably / I suppose" (because really, nine times out of ten that will be the correct answer in Ireland).

The Rise of *Gaeilge* Tattoos With more and more people every day deciding to choose *Gaeilge* and incorporate the language into their lives, tattoos are no exception. Whether as a personal ode to the language or to show others that you love, speak, or appreciate the language, tattoos *as Gaeilge* can be seen all across the globe. The word *dóchas*, meaning "hope," shares its etymology with ***is dócha*** and is a common choice due to its inspiring sentiment.

Is mise ____ / ____ is ainm dom PHRASE

(iss MISH-eh ____) / (____ iss AH-nim dum)

I'm _____ / _____ is my name

Here's your chance to learn how to introduce yourself to a fellow *Gaeilgeoir*. These are two different variations to introduce yourself, an informal and a more formal option. ***Is mise*** (insert name here) is an informal way of saying "I'm (insert name here)." You can use this to introduce yourself in casual settings like at a party, meeting new coworkers, or in social settings. (Insert name here) ***is ainm dom*** can be translated to "(insert name here) is my name," and this phrase is used in formal settings, such as the beginning of a speech or when writing a biographical piece about yourself. Having said that, it's not *incorrect* to use (insert name here) ***is ainm dom*** in informal settings, but it would come across as quite stiff. It's often best to stick with a swift and cheerful ***is mise*** (insert name here) among friends.

Who Do You Belong To? The phrase *cé as thú (kay aws hoo)* is used in Irish to ask someone where they're from, but really it's asking, "Who are you from?" or "What's your family name?" The Irish have a deep-rooted need to establish a connection with others by assessing familial links or mutual connections. For example, "Would you be related to the Murphys from Cork? I went to college with a Murphy from Cork." Nine times out ten, a mutual connection in established.

le cúnamh Dé / le cúnamh breá Dé INTERJECTION

(leh KOO-nah djay / le KOO-nah braw djay)

hopefully; with the help of God

Literally translated, ***le cúnamh Dé*** means "with the help of God," which is an Irish idiom used in the same manner as the word "hopefully." For example, *le cúnamh Dé, beidh an aimsir go deas (leh koo-nah djay bye on ime-shur guh jahs)*, meaning "with the help of God (hopefully), the weather will be nice." If you want to take this phrase a step further, you can enlist God's beautiful help in fulfilling your wishes by adding the adjective *breá*, meaning, of course, "beautiful." Another figurative translation of this phrase is "God willing," similar to the expression *inshallah* in Arabic.

God has appeared in many phrases *as Gaeilge* thus far, such as *Dia duit* (hello) and *buíochas le Dia* (thankfully), so why is "with the help of God" not *le cúnamh Dia*, instead of ***le cúnamh Dé***? The answer is *An Tuiseal Ginideach*—the genitive case—one of the trickiest concepts for learners of the Irish language; it involves altering the spelling of words in certain situations. One of the situations in which *An Tuiseal Ginideach* is used is when two nouns come together. In the phrase ***le cúnamh Dé***, the nouns *cúnamh* (help) and *Dia* (God) come together, meaning that the spelling of *Dia* is slightly altered to *Dé*, as per the genitive case. Hence the phrase ***le cúnamh Dé*** instead of *le cúnamh Dia*.

le do thoil / más é do thoil é INTERJECTION

(lyeh duh hull) / (mawsh ay duh huill ay)

please

If you're a generally well-rounded, good-willed person, saying "please" is likely part of your daily interactions. Therefore, swapping "please" for ***le do thoil*** or ***más é do thoil é*** is a great way to integrate more *Gaeilge* into your life. Both forms figuratively translate to "please," but the shorter form ***le do thoil*** is more commonly used among Irish speakers and rolls off the tongue a bit quicker than ***más é do thoil é***. The noun *toil* means "will," "inclination," or "desire," stemming from the Old Irish word *tol*, which bears the same translation. In the form ***le do thoil***, *le* is the preposition "with" and *do* is the possessive adjective meaning "your." Combined with the noun *toil*, this phrase hence literally translates to "with your will." In the case of ***más é do thoil é***, the literal translation is "if it is your wish."

Pronouncing *L's* and *D's* You've read about various examples of broad or slender *d's* and *t's* in the Irish language thus far, and the letter *l* is another example of a consonant that can be broad or slender. When followed by a slender vowel, like in ***le do thoil***, the first letter *l* rolls into the subsequent sound. Therefore, this phrase is pronounced *(lyeh duh hull)* instead of *(leh duh hull)*. Implementing these pronunciation features properly makes a huge difference to the quality and integrity of your spoken *Gaeilge*.

maidin mhaith | oíche mhaith INTERJECTION

(MAH-jin wawh) | (EE-ha wawh)

good morning | good night

Maidin mhaith and ***oíche mhaith*** are useful phrases to add to your *Gaeilge* database and simple everyday swaps to make. However, note that these phrases are often disliked by *Gaeilge* enthusiasts because they're direct word-for-word translations from English. *Maidin* means "morning," and *oíche* means "night," and you can probably guess what *maith* translates to . . . "good," of course. Therefore, ***maidin mhaith*** and ***oíche mhaith*** are considered to be *Béarlachas* (English idioms that don't really work naturally *as Gaeilge*). Having said that, using ***maidin mhaith*** and ***oíche mhaith*** is largely accepted and understood by all Irish speakers. If like many *Gaeilge* enthusiasts you wish to avoid *Béarlachas*, there is a more formal way of saying "good morning." By combining *Dia duit*, meaning "hello," and *ar maidin*, meaning "this morning," you get *Dia duit ar maidin* as another form of "good morning."

Top of the Morning to Ya . . . ? Funny story, the Irish do NOT say "top of the morning to you." It is believed that the origin of "top of the morning to you" stems from a mistranslation of the greeting *mór na maidine duit. Mór* means "big" or "great" and *na maidine duit* means "of the morning to you." If *mór* was incorrectly translated to "top," it's easy to see how this phrase popped up. Regardless of origins in *Gaeilge* and mistranslations, "top of the morning to you" is a not a phrase in the Irish vernacular.

maith thú PHRASE

(mawh hoo)

well done

Given that the Irish are extremely generous at dishing out praise and encouragement, the phrase ***maith thú*** often rolls off the tongue. As a people, the Irish love to recognize and appreciate the achievements and success of others. ***Maith thú*** has a simple translation, with *maith* meaning "good" and *thú* meaning "you." Therefore, when assembled, you get the straight-to-the-point "good you." This phrase is frequently heard in academic settings and is used by teachers and educators to give praise to students for a job well done. It can also be used in general daily interactions to acknowledge smaller, yet still significant achievements, almost like a symbolic, heartfelt pat on the back. The appropriate response to ***maith thú*** would be *go raibh maith agat* (thank you).

Good on Ya **The most comparable Irish idiom to *maith thú* (apart from "well done" of course) would be "good on ya." This is a more informal phrase and would be used in the context of acknowledging small daily achievements as opposed to more noteworthy successes. Saying "good on ya" to someone reflects having a genuine sense of pride in them and hits extra close to home if paired with an actual pat on the back (not just a symbolic one).**

Mise le meas PHRASE

(MISH-eh leh mass)

Yours truly, with respect

Earlier in this chapter, you may have seen the phrase *beir bua*, meaning "best wishes" (kind of). In the phrase's entry, it was mentioned that you might need some other options in case you don't wish victory and triumph on the recipient of your email. Well, here's your solution. *Mise le meas* directly translates to "It is I, with respect" and it functions in a similar manner to "yours truly," "with regards," or "sincerely." This phrase is another perfect email sign-off but is a tad more formal and less personable—the kind of sign-off you would use in an email to a stranger or to your not-so-favorite coworker. Still professional of course, yet you're not wishing them to bear victory and triumph 'til the end of time.

The origins of the word *meas*, meaning "respect," are hard to track, as it shares little to no similarities to any other language, apart for *Gaeilge*'s close relative, Scottish Gaelic. However, the Irish word *meas* can also refer to an "estimation or judgment," which bears an undeniable likeness to the Old Irish and Proto-Celtic words *mess* and *messus*, both meaning "judgment," "scale," or "measure." Therefore, it is possible that the word *meas* in the Irish language, meaning "respect," developed from the idea of respect being a balancing act that must be upheld by both parties.

Ná bac liom / leis / léi / leo PHRASE

(naw bawk lyum / lesh / lay-hee / lyoh)

Don't mind me / him / her / them

As a nation, the Irish people tend to have a habit of deflecting attention away from themselves; you could say that the Irish are quite humble. The phrase ***ná bac liom***, meaning "don't mind me" or "pay no heed to me," can be used in a multitude of scenarios. For example, if you've gone on a tangent and realize halfway through that the majority of what you're saying makes absolutely no sense, you can segue on out of there with a ***ná bac liom***. If your friend is acting up and you want to excuse them on their behalf, throw out a ***ná bac leis / léi / leo***, "don't mind him / her / them." If something or someone is bothering you, a confidant could tell you to ***ná bac leis*** "pay no heed to it"; in other words, don't give the situation another second's thought.

Tongue Twister An infamous tongue twister, or *rabhlóg (r-ow-loge)* in the Irish language is *Ná bac le mac an bhacaigh is ní bhacaidh mac a bhacaigh leat*, which is (roughly) pronounced as such: *(naw bock leh mawk on wok-ee ihs knee wok-ee mawk ah wok-ee lyat)*. This tongue twister translates to "Don't bother the beggar's son, and the beggar's son won't bother you." Take that, Peter Piper.

sceitimíní NOUN

(SKETCH-ih-MEE-nee)

excitement

There are many instances *as Gaeilge* where the sound of the words seems to echo the sentiment of their meaning; the word ***sceitimíní*** being one of these instances. The assonance in the repeated slender vowels (the *í*'s) gives this word a light and airy feeling, comparable to butterflies felt in one's stomach when excitement strikes. Using this noun in a sentence requires an understanding of how emotions function grammatically in the Irish language. Emotions are frequently used in the context of a state of being that is upon you, or on you. For example, "there is happiness on me" as opposed to "I am happy," "there is hunger on me" as opposed to "I am hungry," and in the case of ***sceitimíní***, "there is excitement on me." Therefore, in Irish, you would use the format *tá sceitimíní orm. Tá* meaning "there is" and *orm* being the prepositional pronoun "on me." This structure really captures the essence of being enveloped in the emotion, and it applies to all emotions and states of being, such as sadness, grief, and others. Also, note that *tá sceitimíní orm* isn't the only way to imply that you are excited in Irish, as the expression *tá mé ar bís*, as previously discussed, meaning "I'm excited / I'm buzzing," is also frequently used among Irish speakers.

sláinte INTERJECTION

(slawn-chah)

cheers; health

If you were to only take one phrase from this book to start integrating into your everyday life, let it be ***sláinte***. Literally translated, the word ***sláinte*** means "health," but it is used in the context of "cheers" when making a toast before a drink. Raising a glass and announcing ***sláinte*** is an invitation for people to join in and share a sense of togetherness and community. It is a representation of the Irish friendliness and hospitality as you wish good health upon those around you and drink together. This is a strong cultural tradition that is practiced not only on Irish soil but across the globe. There are few cities around the world in which you won't find an Irish pub; in fact, it is estimated that there are over 6,500 in total. If you are in a pub on the Emerald Isle, in an Irish pub abroad, or simply in Irish company, saying ***sláinte*** before that first sip is the perfect invitation to those around you to celebrate what's most important in life: good health.

This phrase originally stems from the Old Irish word *slán (slawn)* meaning "sound, healthy and safe" and can be extended to *sláinte mhaith (slawn-cha wawh)*, meaning "good health," or *sláinte 's táinte (slawn-cha ihs tawn-chag)*, meaning "health and wealth." However, in most cases, a simple ***sláinte*** will suffice—you don't want to waste any time before you have a taste of your drink.

slán agat / slán leat INTERJECTION

(slawn aw-gut) / (slawn lyaht)

goodbye

You really thought saying goodbye *as Gaeilge* would be as simple as a one-word farewell? Well, you clearly don't know *Gaeilge* well enough yet, so strap in. You will often see "goodbye" being translated to *slán* but that one word doesn't cut it; there's further context (and prepositions) needed to paint the full picture. Imagine the following scene. You're in a shop and you've just checked out with the shopkeeper. You would say "***slán agat***" to the shopkeeper and the shopkeeper would say "***slán leat***" to you. Now, what's the difference between the two and when are they used? The *agat* in ***slán agat*** is the prepositional pronoun "at" + "you." Therefore, ***slán agat*** is used when saying goodbye to a person who is staying in a given position (the shopkeeper who is staying in place at the register). Think of it like you're throwing the goodbye *at* them. ***Slán leat*** is said to someone who is leaving or walking away from the conversation (you are leaving the shop). The *leat* in ***slán leat*** is the prepositional pronoun "with" + "you." A good way to remember this one is that ***slán leat*** is said to the person who is taking the goodbye *with* them. So just a quick recap; you say "***slán agat***" to the shopkeeper who is staying in their given position, and the shopkeeper says "***slán leat***" to you as you are leaving the shop (and conversation).

tabhair aire INTERJECTION

(TORE AH-reh)

take care; mind yourself

The phrase ***tabhair aire*** truly feels like a comforting, enveloping hug from a warm Irish soul. This is a shortened adaption of the phrase *tabhair aire duit féin*, meaning "take care of yourself," and it is typically used at the end of a conversation when you're parting ways with someone. *Tabhair aire duit féin* has an undeniable level of care and comfort associated with it. Broken down on a linguistic level, *tabhair* is the verb "to give," *aire* is "care" or "attention," *duit* is the prepositional pronoun "to you," and finally *féin* means "oneself." *Aire* is the most interesting word in this phrase, as it can weld a multitude of meanings, most notably being "nobleman or chief" and "Minister of State." A colloquial Irish farewell comparable to *tabhair aire duit féin* is "mind how you go," which essentially means "take care on your way," or "mind yourself now."

So, next time you're bidding *adieu* to a friend or family member, try wrapping up the interaction with a heartfelt *tabhair aire duit féin*. This phrase can also serve as a daily reminder to yourself, to both prioritize and look after none other than yours truly. Make space for the phrase *tabhair aire duit féin* as a mantra in your life to prompt self-care and well-being.

tá brón orm INTERJECTION

(thaw broe-n urm)

I'm sorry

This is another phrase that can be at the heart of discussion and discourse within the Irish-speaking community and, therefore, is worth discussing. In many Irish books and lessons, you will be taught that ***tá brón orm*** translates to "I'm sorry," which isn't entirely true. In the Irish language, people *wear* their emotions. Not in a "wear your heart on your sleeve" sense, but in the grammatical sense. To express an emotion *as Gaeilge*, follow the format *tá* (insert emotion here) *orm*, which means "(insert emotion here) is on me." The word *brón* in ***tá brón orm*** translates to sorrow, so it's understandable why people use the word in the same way that "sorry" is used in English. However, there's a stark difference between being sorry and being sorrowful. For example, if you were to bump into someone by accident, it would be natural to say, "I'm sorry!," but does it make sense to say, "I'm sorrowful!" (***tá brón orm***)? If right were right, ***tá brón orm*** would be exclusively used to express sympathy or understanding of another person's troubles. Having said that, ***tá brón orm*** is largely accepted and used in the same manner as "I'm sorry," but again, it calls up the idea of *Béarlachas*. In some cases, if you wish to avoid an English phrase that compromises *Gaeilge* accuracy, you can use *gabh mo leithsceál* (excuse me) instead.

tá fáilte romhat INTERJECTION

(thaw FAWL-cheh row-ut)

you're welcome

Tá fáilte romhat can be used both as a response to *go raibh maith agat* (thank you) and also to welcome someone into a space. This phrase doesn't leave too much to the imagination and bears a literal, straightforward translation. *Tá* means "is" or "there is," *fáilte* means "welcome," and *romhat* is the prepositional pronoun "before you." Therefore, "there is welcome before you." Like many of the phrases that have been explored thus far, there is a widely used condensed form; for ***tá fáilte romhat***, that comes in the form of just the word *fáilte* on its own. For example, if someone has said "*go raibh maith agat*" (thank you) to you, you can respond with the longer "***tá fáilte romhat***," or simply "*fáilte*" as a conversational or slang alternative. This also applies if you're welcoming someone to a space or an event. If you were to open the door to visitors arriving for a party, you can throw out a warm *fáilte* and follow it up with a *Conas atá tú?* (How are you?). If you wish to express the sentiment of "you're welcome" to more than one person, you simply swap the prepositional *romhat*, meaning "before you," for *romhaibh (row-iv)*, meaning "before you all."

4 Fun and Entertainment

In this chapter, you'll investigate various aspects of Irish culture with a particular spotlight on fun and entertainment. The Irish people have earned a reputation globally as being the life of the party in any social gathering, and rightfully so. As a nation of quick-witted people with a sharp sense of humor, the Irish certainly know how to have fun and provide entertainment to all those blessed to be in their company. Many traditions deeply rooted in the history of the country live on to this day and breathe life into music, sport, and social practices, and much more.

abú INTERJECTION

(ah-BOO)

hup, hooray

The word ***abú*** literally translates to "forever" but can be used in a variety of social circumstances, particularly sporting endeavors. It will most commonly be used as a chant when one wants to cheer on their given county, town, province, or team. For example, if you were from the county of Longford, you would place the word ***abú*** after the name of the county. Exclaiming *Longfort abú* literally translates to "Longford forever," or figuratively translates to "hooray Longford" or "long live Longford." This format applies to all contexts in which ***abú*** is used to cheer on a given sports team. In using this phrase for your team, not only are you expressing everlasting loyalty and support to them, but you are also wishing success upon them. This word is not reserved for *only* sporting endeavors, as it is also used to show support or loyalty to a given cause. A common phrase among the Irish community is *an Ghaeilge abú!*, roughly meaning "long live the Irish language" or "hooray for the Irish language."

Hup The word *hup*, like the marching rhythm, is present both in spoken English and Irish. *Hup* can be used at a music session to cheer on the musicians and add to the liveliness of the atmosphere, to cheer someone on if they need a little pep to their step, or just in general as a casual conversation filler. The opportunities to throw in a *hup* are endless.

ag déanamh an diabhail VERB

(egg jay-nuh on jowil)

doing the devil; up to no good

When describing someone who is simply up to no good, this is the perfect phrase. To be ***ag déanamh an diabhail*** literally translates to "doing the devil," but if you stretch the phrase out, one could infer that it means "doing the devil's work." In the Irish language and culture, bringing the devil into the picture evokes an immediate sense of evil and wickedness, as you might expect. In this phrase, *ag déanamh* is the verb "to be doing" and *an diabhail* refers to, you guessed it, the devil himself.

An interesting note on Hiberno-English is the pronunciation and spelling used when speaking about the devil in informal language in Ireland. The "devil" is referred to as the "divil," which may be a result of the spelling of *an diabhal*. The replacement of the letter *e* with the letter *i* in this spelling trickles through into many other forms. For example, the result or by-product of "doing the devil's work" is "devilment," which refers to mischievous or reckless behavior. In Ireland, the influence from the Irish-language spelling is palpable, leaving you with "divilment." As an Irishism, to call someone a *divil* in a lighthearted manner is to call them a messer, a troublemaker, or someone who's up to no good. Who knew you could get so many variations from one phrase?

ag déanamh gaisce VERB

(egg jay-nuh gosh-keh)

showing off

Whether it be in sports, music, work, or social settings, there's always a possibility of encountering a show-off. When you do encounter such behavior, ***ag déanamh gaisce*** is the perfect phrase to use to call it out—either publicly or privately, up to you. The word *gaisce* by itself can yield a litany of meanings, some of which include "achievement," "gloating," "heroism," and "bragging." When followed by the verb *ag déanamh*, meaning "to do," this phrase figuratively translates to "showing off," but the literal translation refers to someone "making an achievement" of themselves. A person who is ***ag déanamh gaisce*** is doing everything possible to draw attention toward themselves, projecting a heightened or inflated perception of their skills and talents (or lack thereof).

Notions, Notions, Notions In Ireland, a way of calling out someone's over-the-top efforts is to say they have "notions." As previously discussed, the country has a reputation of having a debilitating case of small-town mindset. If someone is to step outside the box, whether it be in terms of fashion, career choices, or personal feats, they will be brandished as having "notions." Oh, someone bought a designer handbag? Notions. You're going to Vegas for your birthday? Notions. In essence, having "notions" is possibly the worst thing a person could possess. But don't let that stop you; this is a dying perception among younger generations.

ag spaisteoireacht VERB

(egg spash-tore-ukt)

sauntering; rambling

Going ***ag spaisteoireacht*** is the perfect activity to add to a laid-back Sunday itinerary. There are many words in English that can be used to describe this idea. To go ***ag spaisteoireacht*** is to go rambling, sauntering, or promenading and is an exquisite way to describe a casual stroll. Many words and phrases *as Gaeilge* contain deeper meanings than just the literal translation. In the case of ***ag spaisteoireacht***, the verb incorporates the idea of a very particular type of walk or stroll in which you feel free and light. The letter combinations evoke a light and airy feeling, comparable to aspects of nature. At the onset of *spaisteoireacht*, the *(ahh)* sound is reminiscent of a light breeze while the *(shhh)* sound brings the sounds of gushing water to your mind. Given this, it would feel morally and linguistically wrong to use the phrase ***ag spaisteoireacht*** to describe any kind of walk other than those in which you are aimlessly strolling through nature, only focusing on being present in the moment. The origins of this phrase can be linked to the Latin word *spatior*, which is the verb used to describe walking about. To change this phrase into a noun to describe someone who would often find themself to be ***ag spaisteoireacht***, the ending *-eacht* can be removed; this leaves you with the noun *spaisteoir*, "a stroller, saunterer, or promenader."

amadán NOUN

(aw-mah-dawn)

idiot; fool

The infamous ***amadán***; you either love them or hate them. The word ***amadán*** in the Irish language refers to a "fool" or "idiot," and it can be used playfully or as a full-blown insult, depending on the tone and delivery. The Irish people aren't shy of dishing out insults (when deserved, of course), and it's common to call someone an ***amadán*** when they're acting foolish. Comparative colloquial phrases in English used in the same context as ***amadán*** would be "eejit," "gobshite," or "gombeen."

The word ***amadán*** itself stems from the tales of the *amadán dubh (aw-mah-dawn duv)*, meaning "dark fairy" or "dark fool" in Irish mythology and folklore. The *amadán dubh* is depicted as being a mischievous character who incited madness and oblivion. It's said that those perceived to be insane or to see things that others don't were touched by the *amadán dubh*. This creature was said to be one of the most powerful fairies of all and would haunt the hillside at nightfall, playing his reed pipes in an eerie, mischievous manner to entice souls unlucky enough to cross paths with him. The touch of the *amadán dubh* was just as terrifying as his face, as a stroke from this creature would leave people paralyzed and insane. So, in other words, calling someone an ***amadán*** carries just as much, if not more, historical significance as it does cultural.

Ar mhaith leat a bheith curtha le mo mhuintir? PHRASE

(air wah lyat ah veh curha leh muh WIN-tir)

Would you like to be buried with my family?

If you find yourself in a social setting surrounded by Irish speakers and you happen to come across someone who tickles your fancy, you need to have a pickup line or two ready to go. And is there anything more alluring than discussing future burial plans? As far as *Gaeilge* is concerned, maybe not. Although this might not be the most romantic pickup line, it's certainly attention-grabbing. In asking someone ***Ar mhaith leat a bheith curtha le mo mhuintir?***, you are insinuating that you like them so much that you see yourselves married and, ultimately, having an amalgamated burial.

That's enough about the romance; time for some linguistic analysis. In this expression, *ar mhaith leat* means "would you like," *a bheith* means "to be," and *curtha* is the verbal adjective of the verb *cuir*, "to put." When discussing burial *as Gaeilge*, the verb *cuir* is used in reference to literally being "put" into the ground. To wrap up this pickup line, the phrase *le mo mhuintir* translates to "with my community/family." So, ditch the "Do you come here often?" and take the more direct approach with ***Ar mhaith leat a bheith curtha le mo mhuintir?***

bothántaíocht NOUN

(buh-hawn-thee-ukh)

visiting houses

The tradition of ***bothántaíocht*** is a cherished Irish tradition that encapsulates the spirit of the island of Ireland and its people. This practice involves making the rounds in your town or village and visiting from house to house to share stories, gossip, wisdom, and knowledge. ***Bothántaíocht*** gives life to the importance of face-to-face interactions and real-life human connections. Avid supporters of ***bothántaíocht*** would shudder at the sight of modern-day practices such as social media, Zoom, FaceTime, and voice messages. This practice captured the ways in which people enriched relationships by spending intentional quality time together and bonding through spoken word. Tales from previous generations would be passed down, shared, and preserved, but ***bothántaíocht*** also served to keep people in the loop about the most recent ongoings and gossip, because who doesn't love a good intimate gossiping session.

The Back Door Traditionally, it would be very rare for a loved one to use the front door. Someone appearing at the front door instills dread, as it couldn't possibly be a friendly visit. A friend coming for a casual visit would have let themselves in the back door. Given that the kitchen (and therefore the kettle to make a cup of tea) would typically be at the back of the house, the back door is a far more intimate and personal means of entry and thus another concept that captures the welcoming spirit of the Irish.

caitheadh cruife NOUN

(caw-ha KRI-fah)

horseshoe pitching

A horseshoe can have many functions—most notably as a symbol of good luck and protection and, of course, to protect a horse's hoof. However, this metal object served another purpose in a historic Irish practice that has been preserved to this day. The practice of ***caitheadh cruife***, or horseshoe pitching, was a game played traditionally at crossroads in Counties Wexford, Carlow, Laois, and Kildare. Sessions of this game could take upward of eight hours to complete, and some believe men used this game as an excuse to avoid their families while drinking. This game can also be referred to as "meggars" in Ireland, and it involves throwing horseshoes toward a stake in the ground with the intention of encircling the stake or getting the horseshoe as close as possible.

The Lucky Irish Horseshoe In many cultures, horseshoes are hung in an upside-down letter *u* position to ensure the good luck spills out over anyone who passes underneath. However, in Irish culture it is believed that an upside-down letter *u* horseshoe is unlucky, as the good luck has been wasted. Instead, you'll find horseshoes hung in an upright letter *u* position above many doors and entryways in Ireland.

caith siar é agus ná lig aniar é PHRASE

(cah sheer awgis ay naw lig A-neer ay)

throw it back and don't throw it up

No, this phrase doesn't refer to physically throwing something backward. This is a phrase that can be used as a toast with friends, and it literally translates to "throw it back and don't throw it up." This phrase refers to throwing the drink down your throat with the subsequent hope that it won't make you sick. It is important to understand the circumstances in which it would be a great idea to use this phrase and when it might be best to avoid it. For example, if you're at a friend's twenty-first birthday party, ***caith siar é agus ná lig aniar é*** would suit the environment. Refreshments at Christmas with your grandparents? Might be best to stick with some of the tamer toast options from Chapter 3.

Midnight Munch From 1935 to 2000, businesses in Ireland who had late night licenses to serve alcohol were required to serve a substantial meal to all nightclub goers at midnight. That's right, the music would be lowered, the lights would be turned up, and dinner would be served. At midnight. Whether or not any of the nightclub goers ate the meal, businesses were legally required to provide the food; but regardless, it's safe to say this scheme definitely helped many to ***caith siar é agus ná lig aniar é***.

caochta ADJECTIVE

(cwee-ukh-tah)

blind drunk

The term ***caochta*** should be reserved for specific circumstances. On the surface, it is used to express being drunk, but if you've learned anything from this book so far, you should know that it goes much deeper than that. If you're ***caochta***, you're not just drunk, you're blind drunk; the verging-on-blackout kind of drunk. As an adjective, ***caochta*** can also mean just "blind," not "blind drunk," which is comparable to the Latin word *caecus*, also meaning "blind." As a verb, *caoch* means "to wink" and as a noun, a *caoch* is a person who is blind in one eye or a blind creature. Talk about versatility.

The Drunken Irish Although "The Drunken Irish" is a stereotype this book won't prove or disprove, the Irish certainly have plenty of slang words for "drunk." Some examples are scuttered, plastered, baloobas, ossified, flutered, stocious, paralytic, gone, langers, locked, twisted, jarred (or well-jarred), bananas, full as a bingo bus, in a hape, in a hoop, in bits, mangled, mouldy, off my trolley, or out of my tree. So, next time you or someone in your vicinity has had a few too many, swap out "drunk" for one of the more flamboyant Irishisms just described.

cead NOUN

(khad)

traditional sport

On the picturesque Aran Islands off the west coast of Ireland, the traditional sport of ***cead*** is preserved. This sport can only be played on St. Patrick's Day, and practicing throughout the year in preparation for the big day is strictly forbidden. The yearly ***cead*** tournament is held on *Inis Meáin (inish myawn)*, the middle island of the Aran Islands, and the rules are pretty straightforward. Men carve wooden bats for the game and the ***cead*** itself, a smaller piece of wood, functions as the ball. The ***cead*** is placed against a flat stone, then hit into the air, and finally hit again hard and fast while it's airborne past a rope that's over 30 meters away. This historic game requires skill and precision. Because the islanders are forbidden from practicing year-round, the game illustrates that culture and traditions live within people, just as the skills of ***cead*** live within the population of *Inis Meáin*.

Inisherin The Oscar-nominated movie *The Banshees of Inisherin* starring Barry Keoghan, Colin Farrell, and Brendan Gleeson was filmed between two islands off the west coast of Ireland: Achill Island and *Inis Mór*. Achill Island is off the coast of County Mayo, and *Inis Mór* is the largest of the Aran Islands off the coast of County Galway. The island Inisherin in the movie doesn't exist, but the name bears an uncanny resemblance to *Inis Oírr (inish ear)*, the smallest of the Aran Islands.

céilí NOUN

(kay-lee)

social gathering

A ***céilí*** is an Irish social event or gathering where you can expect to see traditional dancing and music. Appropriately named, the dancing found at a ***céilí*** is referred to as ***céilí*** dancing, and the bands that play music at a ***céilí*** are called a ***céilí*** band. That's easy to remember! ***Céilí*** dancing is a style of group dance and can follow various forms: couples dances, four in front of four, a line of men facing a line of women, and much more. Some of these dances date back to the 1500s and have been passed down through generations, while new generations are also choreographing new styles of ***céilí*** dancing. A traditional ***céilí*** band consists of ten instruments including the accordion, the concertina (a smaller instrument like an accordion), harmonica, uilleann pipes (similar to the Scottish bagpipes), banjo, fiddle (another word for violin, but specific to Irish, bluegrass, and other types of music), flute, tin whistle, drums, and piano. Traditionally, the ***céilí*** band would have needed to be able to play loud enough to be heard by the dancers over the noise from the spectators and others in attendance at the ***céilí***. With the help of amplification, this challenge isn't as pressing for ***céilí*** bands now. A renowned ***céilí*** band is the Kilfenora Céilí Band. Note: ***Céilí*** can be used to refer to any kind of lively social gathering in Ireland; it's not strictly reserved for ***céilí*** bands and dancing.

ciorcal comhrá NOUN

(CYUR-kill coe-raw)

conversation circle

A ***ciorcal comhrá*** leaves little to the imagination in both its translation and what it entails. *Ciorcal* means "circle," and *comhrá* means "conversation." Therefore, a ***ciorcal comhrá*** is a "conversation circle." A ***ciorcal comhrá*** is organized by Irish speakers as an opportunity to come together and speak the language in an informal social setting. Many people in Ireland don't use the language for work, school/college, or in their broader social circles, meaning opportunities to use the language in a practical sense with other Irish speakers can be difficult to find. These events create an open, welcoming space for both learners and fluent speakers. Anyone can host a ***ciorcal comhrá***, and anyone can participate; there are no rules. So, why don't you try organizing a ***ciorcal comhrá*** either virtually or in-person with those who also have an interest in *Gaeilge*?

Pop-Up *Gaeltacht* The "Pop-Up *Gaeltacht*" is a phrase that has been coined to refer to events in which Irish speakers come together in the name of speaking the language. The *Gaeltacht* regions in Ireland are the areas in which *Gaeilge* is the predominantly spoken language. Therefore, an organized Irish-speaking event that is held outside the *Gaeltacht* is referred to as a "Pop-Up *Gaeltacht*." Whether it be in New York, Sydney, Canada, or Dubai, wherever the Irish are, you will find a "Pop-Up *Gaeltacht*."

cluichí Gaelacha NOUN

(kli-hee gway-luch-ah)

Gaelic games

If you plan on visiting Ireland, you must squeeze seeing a Gaelic game into the itinerary. The ***cluichí Gaelacha*** consist of six different sports: hurling, Gaelic football, handball, rounders, camogie, and ladies' football. Hurling is an extremely fast-paced and fierce stick and ball sport; think of a mix of lacrosse, hockey, and baseball. Gaelic football can be compared to a mix of American football and soccer and is predominantly referred to in Ireland as just "football." Handball is played in a court or an alley whereby players strike a small ball against a wall, and it can be played in either doubles or singles. Rounders is a bat and ball game and bears the most similarities to baseball; it's generally accepted that baseball derives from rounders in one way or another. Camogie refers to the ladies' teams who play hurling, and ladies' football is Gaelic football. These games are played all over Ireland by both young and old, and they play a huge role in Irish culture, traditions, and social practices.

The Skort Debacle Until May 2025, women who played camogie were required to wear a skort instead of the infamous GAA shorts (as made famous by Paul Mescal) to participate in the sport. Camogie players around the country and allies came together to make their stand against the archaic rule of skort wearing, and as a result, a rule was passed that allows camogie players to choose between GAA shorts or the skort.

cúlchaint NOUN

(cool-k-eye-nch)

gossip

Like everyone else, Irish people love good gossip. Not only is gossiping a guilty pleasure for the Irish, but the Irish language bares the juiciest word to describe the practice: ***cúlchaint***. Interestingly, the linguistic breakdown of the word is just as, if not more, scandalous than the practice itself. ***Cúlchaint*** is a compound word and can be broken down into the individual segments of *cúl* and *chaint*. *Cúl* translates to "back" and *caint* translates to "talk" or "chat" (you see where this is going). Therefore, ***cúlchaint*** literally and figuratively translates to "talking about someone behind their back." This word is easily adaptable to refer to someone as a gossiper. Simply add *-eoir* to the end of ***cúlchaint***, leaving you with *cúlchainteoir*. So, next time you have some juicy information to divulge to your friend, swap out "gossip" for ***cúlchaint*** and be your truest, shameless *cúlchainteoir* self.

***-eoir* / *-óir* Suffix** The *-eoir* and *-óir* suffixes in the Irish language denote someone who specializes in or is renowned for a particular thing. For example, a *fiaclóir* (*fiacail* = tooth + *-óir*) is a dentist, a *Gaeilgeoir* (*Gaeilge* = Irish + *-eoir*) is an Irish speaker, and a *múinteoir* (*múin* = to teach + *-eoir*) is a teacher.

cuma na maitheasa PHRASE

(KUHM-ah nah MAWH-iss-ah)

the look of health

There's no shortage of situations in which the phrase ***cuma na maitheasa*** can be used. For example, if someone is acting a bit sluggish and you need them to kick it up a notch, you can tell them to put ***cuma na maitheasa*** on themselves. The equivalent colloquial phrase to this sentiment in informal English would be telling someone "to get their butt/bum in gear." ***Cuma na maitheasa*** can also be used to refer to something that looks impressive. For example, *tá cuma na maitheasa ar an teach (taw KUHM-ah nah MAWH-iss-ahh air on chock)*, meaning "the house looks impressive." If you simply want to tell someone they're looking good or looking well, you can say *tá cuma na maitheasa ort (taw KUMH-ah na MAWH-iss-ah urt)*. You may also use the phrase ***cuma na maitheasa*** when you start to come back to life after a hangover. The headache and nausea have retreated and the color is starting to come back to your face. At that point, ***cuma na maitheasa*** is upon you.

The Cure Both in Irish and Mexican culture, the term "the cure" is used as an alternative to the phrase "the hair of the dog" when referring to having a drink the following day in an effort to cure your hangover. In Ireland, many people will also often say they're going for a "healer" drink.

dallamullóg NOUN

(daw-lah-mull-ohg)

deception; hoax; mislead

Dallamullóg is one of the most musical, fun-sounding words in the Irish language. In a figurative sense, the word refers to a deception, to mislead someone, or a hoax. In a literal sense, there's much more beneath the surface. ***Dallamullóg*** is a compound word, with the first unit being *dall*, meaning "blind." The phrase "to pull the wool over someone's eyes" is used to express the idea of deception or misleading someone, and this stems from medieval times. At medieval fairs, robbers would pull their victim's hood over their eyes while they cut their purse strings and stole from them. It's from this practice that the phrase "to pull the wool over someone's eyes" arises. In doing so, you are blinding the victim of deception and hindering their sight to ensure they can't see what you're actually up to. Therefore, the *dall* (blind) in ***dallamullóg*** refers to either the person you're deceiving being blind as to your true intentions, or the fact that you're blinding them and hiding the real truth of your actions from them.

damhsa seit NOUN

(DOWS-ah set)

set dancing

Damhsa seit is another form of traditional Irish dancing that has been around for over one hundred fifty years and is still practiced to this day. The style of dance itself originates from the French quadrille dance, a dance that was performed by four couples in rectangular formation, which was then brought to Ireland by the English armies from the 1780s onward. Every dance or "set" is comprised of shorter individual "figures" that are danced in succession to traditional Irish tunes, such as jigs, reels, hornpipes, and polkas. Given that this style of dancing requires eight dancers (four couples) to perform a set, it requires social interaction, an aspect that is strengthened by the "change partner" figure that is seen in many sets. This can also be referred to as the "flirtation" figure, and it calls for the couples to exchange partners while dancing and share a brief dance together before returning to their original partners.

Damhsa seit was undocumented before the 1980s, which caused isolated areas to develop their own styles. So, many regions have their own distinct styles of ***damhsa seit*** as well that are named after the area. Dancers take great pride in performing the set of their given region. Some examples include the Connemara set and the Moycullen set hailing from County Galway, and the West Kerry set.

dána ADJECTIVE

(dhawn-ah)

naughty; cheeky; bold

The word **dána** can be used to describe someone who is naughty, cheeky, or bold. There's also an element of *divilment* (devilishness) at play with **dána** that incorporates mischievous behavior and lighthearted fun, as opposed to the solely negative connotation of the word "naughty." ***Dána*** is flung around households and classrooms in Ireland with parents telling their children and teachers telling their students to *ná bí dána! (naw bee dhawn-ah)*—"don't be bold!" If you're out and about with your friends or in a social setting, **dána** can be used in a more fun sense as opposed to in a disciplinary sense. If you're feeling mischievous and want to stir the pot, you could say you're feeling **dána**. If your friend is chatting someone up at the bar, you could call them **dána**. If they've had a bit too much to drink and are getting rowdy, that would also constitute being **dána**. If you turn around and see them dancing on a table, that would most definitely warrant calling out **dána**. So, this is a word that can be thrown out in a variety of circumstances, and depending on the tone and delivery, the intended message can change drastically.

deoch an dorais NOUN

(juk on DUHR-ish)

a drink of the door

Often, an Irish person has insisted that they're leaving the pub, attempted an escape, and yet found themself in the exact same position a number of hours later. The generous Irish nature means further cups of tea, stories, and drinks will be offered when you try to leave, resulting in a longer visit. That last drink that you know you probably don't need and equally shouldn't have is referred to as ***deoch an dorais***, literally translating to "drink of the door." Whether you're being enticed to stay for "just one more" by your friends, or you've gotten too comfy on your chair, there's always room for a ***deoch an dorais***. It's no surprise that this has become a common practice due to the cozy nature of Irish pubs; imagine being sat at the bar beside the open fire and it's raining cats and dogs outside. It's much easier to commit to a ***deoch an dorais*** than it is to face the elements.

One for the Road Although the Irish language has "the drink of the door," Irish English has "the drink for the road." The first drunk-driving laws were introduced in Ireland in 1933, but the law stated only to not drive while "drunk," which left a lot of wiggle room in the perception of what actually constituted "drunk." Amendments were made to the drink-driving act in 1968, which is still the basis of road traffic law in Ireland.

Dhá Phub Déag na Nollag NOUN

(gaww fub djayg nah null-ug)

the Twelve Pubs of Christmas

An Irish Christmas celebration would be so boring without the tradition of the Twelve Pubs of Christmas. Shortened to "the Twelve Pubs," this is a Christmas pub crawl in which a group visits and has one drink in twelve pubs in one night, in succession. Typically, there's a rule or challenge associated with each pub on the journey. Some examples:

- You must only drink your beverage from your nondominant hand
- No phones allowed
- Everyone must speak with a different accent
- Walk backward to the next pub
- You must use fake names for everyone in the group

If you break the rule in a given pub, you must complete a punishment by downing your drink. In cities and bigger towns, it's easier to compile a route and visit twelve pubs in succession, but in smaller towns, groups will usually return to the same pubs until they've completed twelve stops. The first documentation of this tradition was in 1998 in an article by the *Irish Independent* newspaper, which depicted a group of men getting together to embark on a twelve-stop pub crawl on Grafton Street in the country's capital, Dublin.

Fad saoil, gob fliuch, agus bás in Éirinn PHRASE

(fawd seal, gub fluch aw-gis bawss in AIR-inn)

Long life, wet mouth, and death in Ireland

While this may be one of the wackier toasts *as Gaeilge*, it's certainly one of the most fun. ***Fad saoil, gob fliuch, agus bás in Éirinn*** literally translates to "Long life, wet mouth/beak, death in Ireland." That's quite the mouthful, literally and figuratively. *Fad saoil* meaning "long life" is self-explanatory, while *gob fliuch* refers to the wish that you may always have a drink in your hand and therefore in your mouth. *Bás in Éirinn*, meaning "death in Ireland," may seem slightly morbid on the surface but is in actuality a devout display of patriotism and loyalty to one's country. Although this toast may require a tad extra practice to memorize and recite while drinking, it is well worth the dedication. Using ***Fad saoil, gob fliuch, agus bás in Éirinn*** as opposed to ***sláinte*** as a toast will distinguish between the learners and the *Gaeilge* experts.

feis NOUN

(fesh)

competition

The word ***feis*** translates to "festival," but it is most frequently used to describe an Irish dancing competition. If you have partaken in competitive Irish dancing, hearing the word ***feis*** either awakens a sense of excitement or sheer dread in you. The atmosphere at an Irish dancing ***feis*** is loud, exhilarating, overwhelming, crowded, and chaotic, but it is balanced with the love and appreciation for the practice that is palpable in the atmosphere. *Feiseanna (fesh-ih-nah)* (plural) are held across the globe with Irish dancers competing in a variety of categories. Dancers are accompanied by traditional Irish music and dance the styles of reels, treble reels, jigs, slip jigs, light jigs, and hornpipes. Some dances are performed in what's called a light shoe, comparable to a ballet slipper, while others are performed in a hard shoe, comparable to a tap-dancing shoe. The tradition of the ***feis*** or *feiseanna* has gained notoriety for the flamboyancy of dancers' outfits. From fake tan to sparkly dresses and curly wigs, the style is eye-catching.

Dancing Around the Globe The vast number of Irish dancing clubs and societies around the globe stands testament not only to the world's love and appreciation for Irish culture but also to the ability of the Irish to spread said culture. According to the World Irish Dance Association, there are over one hundred forty Irish dancing schools across twenty-one countries.

fiáin ADJECTIVE

(fee-aaw-in)

wild

The next time you want to describe someone, an event, or an atmosphere as being "wild," you can use the word ***fiáin*** instead. The word ***fiáin*** carries an almost disheveled, unkept sentiment and can also be translated to "feral," "fierce," "unruly," "untamed," or "uncultivated." In other words, if something or someone is ***fiáin***, all sense of order has gone out the window. For example, if someone were to ask you, "How was the party last night?," you could respond with, "It was ***fiáin***!"

In reclaiming the word ***fiáin***, the Irish are reclaiming the stereotypes placed on the nation by the early British colonizers. The native Irish people were describe as being "wild" or "barbaric" and many largely overexaggerated descriptions of the people followed. The Irish traditions and customs were seen as barbarous: an internal flame that the English wanted to quench in their first colony.

Na Fianna **_Na Fianna (nah fee-ah-nah)_ were a group of fierce, wild warriors in Irish mythology. To be a member of _Na Fianna_, you not only had to be strong but also highly intelligent. As a group, they were answerable to the High Kings and served to protect the land and Gaelic order. These young men had to go through a vigorous testing process to prove they were worthy of becoming a member of _Na Fianna_. This screening consisted of tests of intelligence, defense, speed, movement, bravery, and chivalry.**

Fleadh Cheoil na hÉireann NOUN

(flaa CYOH-il nah HAIR-inn)

music festival of Ireland

How could a person talk about Irish fun and entertainment without mentioning ***Fleadh Cheoil na hÉireann***, the epitome of culture and craic? The word *fleadh* itself simply refers to a "festival" or a "feast"; *fleadh cheoil* is a "music festival"; and finally, *na hÉireann*, "of Ireland." So, this phrase refers to the "music festival of Ireland."

Fleadh Cheoil na hÉireann is the world's largest traditional Irish music festival. Each year, a town is chosen to host the festival, and thousands attend for the music, song, dance, culture, tradition, and chaos. Regional and provincial *fleadhs* are held countrywide in the lead-up to ***Fleadh Cheoil na hÉireann*** to determine which competitors will progress to the national level of the competition. Blossoming musicians from as young as twelve years of age can compete; many grow up within the organization, partaking yearly. The first national traditional Irish music festival was held in 1951, and this stronghold has expanded every year since.

The National Emblem of Ireland The Irish harp is the national emblem and is seen in branding and logos, like the Guinness logo. Ireland has a rich harping tradition that dates back to the first harp festival in Granard, County Longford in 1781. The harping tradition in Ireland was fostered by wealthy families, as harpists provided entertainment during banquets and formal meals.

griangrafadóireacht NOUN

(GREENgrafa-dhoor-ukt)

photography

Coming in at a whopping twenty letters, ***grianghrafadóireacht*** is (pretty much) the longest word in the Irish language. Knowing this term is a way to show off in front of Irish speakers, or win a game of scrabble—whatever tickles your fancy. In mastering both the spelling and the pronunciation, you're guaranteed to *wow*. The translation of ***grianghrafadóireacht***, however, isn't as impressive as its length, as it means "photography." There is some debate and discussion surrounding ***grianghrafadóireacht*** being the longest word in the Irish language, as it is contested by loanwords such as *deindreacroineolaíocht*, which comes in at twenty-two letters, meaning "dendrochronology." As *deindreacroineolaíocht* is a loanword from English, it's not considered inherently *Gaelach*, as no such word has historically existed in the language. Instead, it's a modern-day adaption to fulfill advancing language requirements and developments. So, perhaps, ***grianghrafadóireacht*** takes the crown.

Muckanaghederdauhaulia The longest place name in Ireland is Muckanaghederdauhaulia, a town in County Galway. This is an anglicized adaption of the original place names *as Gaeilge*: *Muiceanach idir Dhá Sháile*, which literally translates to "pig-marsh between two sea inlets" and makes perfect sense. It's safe to say native English speakers would struggle to pronounce Muckanaghederdauhaulia, making this a perfect example of colonialism butchering language integrity.

leathbhádóir NOUN

(lah-vaw-dhoor)

partner in crime

Who would be complete without their ***leathbhádóir***? A phrase in English that carries the same sentiment as ***leathbhádóir*** could be "partner in crime" or "significant other," depending on the context. However, the term *as Gaeilge* is far more beautiful and meaningful. ***Leathbhádóir*** literally translates to "half boatman," but it gets mushy if you dive into the figurative translation. Think of your ***leathbhádóir*** as your partner, rowing with you and helping you navigate the waters of life. This is someone with whom you are in sync; like two halves of a whole, one oar each. To keep the boat afloat and moving forward, you both need to row to the same rhythm; cooperation and communication are paramount to turning the boat or moving in a new direction.

Leathbhádóir can be used for those you have a romantic or platonic connection with. It can be a term of endearment for your significant other, and in that case, ***leathbhádóir*** would translate to "significant other" or "better half." When using ***leatbhádóir*** to refer to a friend, it is most similar to "partner in crime." To refer to someone as your ***leathbhádóir***, simply add the possessive adjective *mo (muh)*, meaning "my," before it, leaving you with *mo leathbhádóir*.

lúibíní NOUN

(loo-bee-knee)

traditional Irish poetic verses

Lúibíní is a traditional style of Irish-language song or poetry that includes two people exchanging short verses back and forth. When performed, this style follows a traditional pattern, and it balances between singing and melodic dialogue. Both parties will perform the chorus together and will alternate between verses. The term ***lúibíní*** stems from the root word *lúb*—meaning a "loop," a "bend," or "twists." ***Lúibíní***, therefore, would literally translate to "small loops, bends, or twists," which mirrors the back-and-forth style of the performance where the narration bounces between both performers.

The themes of ***lúibíní*** are often comedic and lighthearted, and they can involve an aspect of banter and bickering between both performers. Current political and cultural scandals are a popular theme for ***lúibíní***, with the lyrics poking fun at those in power. Given the topical (and sometimes controversial) nature of these performances, many are never recorded, yet they retain local notoriety. Within the verses, one performer will propose a challenge or issue that the other performer must respond to in their following verse by means of producing a comeback. Those who perform ***lúibíní*** are renowned for being powerful storytellers, and their witty interactions captivate audiences of any size. Note: ***Lúibíní*** also commonly means "parentheses."

póit NOUN

(POE-ch)

excessive amounts of alcohol; hangover

The dreaded ***póit***—an experience that nobody wants to fall victim to. This word directly translates to "an excessive amount of alcohol," but it's figuratively used to refer to a hangover. Like the majority of emotions or states of being *as Gaeilge*, a **póit** is something that is on you or upon you. Therefore, the format *tá* + (emotion/state) + *orm* is used. In this case, you would say *tá póit orm*. Slight spelling adaptions can take this word and form it into units of alternate meaning in the Irish language, all revolving around the drinking of alcohol. For example, a *pótaire (poe-tur-ah)* is someone who drinks excessively, *pótaireacht (poe-tur-ukt)* is the act of drinking excessively, and finally *poitín* (which is the next entry).

As Shook As a Hand at Mass A common colloquial Irish phrase used to describe a hangover is to say either yourself or someone else is "as shook as a hand at mass." A hand will get shaken vigorously during mass, specifically during the Sign of Peace ritual whereby the congregation will be invited to shake hands with each other. If your hangover has gotten to a point where you have no choice but to describe yourself as being "as shook as a hand at mass," the prognosis isn't great.

poitín NOUN

(PUH-cheen)

traditional distilled beverage

Poitín is a traditional Irish alcoholic beverage distilled from potatoes. Distilling this beverage was illegal from 1661 to 1997, but ***poitín*** has come a long way since its days of being produced in secret. The ban on ***poitín*** production was just another portion of the long list of laws instated to suppress Irish culture and traditions. Many Irish people have heard of a local person who makes illicit ***poitín*** or may have even acquired a bottle themselves under mysterious circumstances. But you don't query the ***poitín*** fairies when a bottle lands on your doorstep.

Given that ***poitín*** was illegal for over three hundred years, many shy away from getting this alcohol, and many are unaware that it is now completely legal to produce with a special license. The now legal production of ***poitín*** must comply with some strict regulations: it must be a clean, clear spirit that retains the natural flavors and aromas of the raw materials used in the distilling process. However, this drink will knock your socks off, as it has a minimum of 40 percent alcohol and a maximum of 90 percent. ***Poitín*** is distilled in copper stills that are placed over the open flames of a turf (peat) fire, as per the traditional practice. The smoky flavor comes through in the drink; some feel connected to history and to the land from that very first sip.

port NOUN

(purt)

a tune

In modern-day Irish usage, the word ***port*** refers to a "melody" and in colloquial Irish English, a "tune." Both ***port*** and "tune" are used to describe a song played typically by traditional Irish musicians, and these words will be heard thrown around by both the musicians and audience at a *seisiún ceoil*, a music session. At a *seisiún ceoil*, the participants and musicians will be encouraged to perform a ***port*** and can be heard saying to each other, "*Seinnfimid cúpla port!*" *(shine-ih-meed cooplah purt)*, meaning, "Let's play a few tunes!"

However, in the seventeenth century, the word ***port*** was used in reference to a specific kind of instrumental music performed on the traditional harp both in Ireland and in Gaelic neighbor Scotland. At this time, the great families would have their own specific familial ***port*** that would incidentally be both named after them and dedicated to them. For example, the word ***port*** followed by the family name. Many compositions and recordings of the infamous ***port*** of this time can be attributed to Ruairí Dall Ó Catháin, a blind harpist and composer who was born in Ireland and lived and worked in Scotland. However, many debate whether Ruairí Dall existed at all; his legacy lives on through oral tradition and stories as he has left no written trace in contemporary records.

raiméis NOUN

(raaw-maysh)

nonsense; rigmarole

If you get stuck chatting to someone who is spewing pure and utter ***raiméis***, you want to develop an exit strategy quickly. If someone is chatting ***raiméis***, they are chatting pure and utter nonsense. Their contributions to the conversation have little to no purpose and quite frankly, they are just talking for the sake of talking. The word ***raiméis*** gives the same energy as "blah blah blah"; they can keep blathering on but really, they're benefiting no one, not even themselves. Oftentimes, ***raiméis*** will spill out of a person's mouth toward the end of the night after quite a few drinks have been had. Then, the word vomit begins. You start confessing your love to your best friend, griping about coworkers, and trauma dumping. To be frank, the world would be a better place with ***raiméis*** detectors that would sound a blaring alarm and bring people back to their senses. No one wants to get stuck chatting to the person at the end of the night who is spewing ***raiméis*** and therefore burning the ear off them. However, there are two sides to every story and some could say that nonsense is the spice of life. In that case, it is important to be self-aware, be able to pull the trigger, and cut the ***raiméis*** when it gets to a point of no return.

rírá agus ruaille buaille NOUN

(ree-raw aw-gis rooleh booleh)

commotion; uproar; chaos

Rírá agus ruaille buaille is one of the most fun phrases in the Irish language. You can conceptualize what ***rírá agus ruaille buaille*** encompasses simply by the way it rolls off the tongue. In the dictionary, ***rírá agus ruaille buaille*** is translated to "commotion, uproar, and chaos"; however, a simple translation doesn't do this phrase justice. ***Rírá agus ruaille buaille*** is more of a palpable atmosphere, similar to the old cartoon animations of a smoke cloud and explosions that materialize when a fight erupts in the saloon. A comparable phrase in English would be "all hell breaking loose." However, like many phrases in Irish, ***rírá agus ruaille buaille*** is multifunctional and doesn't always have a negative connotation; it can also refer to a happy and entertaining level of chaos.

rógaire NOUN

(ROE-gir-ah)

rascal

To call someone a ***rógaire*** can either be playful and lighthearted, or it can have a more negative connotation. In the playful sense, a ***rógaire*** refers to a silly rascal who has no bad intentions with their actions. A commonly heard example of Hiberno-English in Ireland that stems from the Irish word ***rógaire*** is "rogue." Many Irish mammies and grannies would be heard calling someone "a lovable *aul* (old) rogue." In calling someone this, you're implying that you're aware of their sometimes-questionable actions but because they mean no harm, you love them anyway. Similarly, a "messer" or a "monkey" is used to describe someone who is often up to mischief but again, their behavior poses no real threat or consequence. Therefore, you're calling them out for what they are, but it doesn't affect your moral view of them. However, if you're not so trusting of someone's behavior, calling them a ***rógaire*** in that context can most definitely have a negative connotation. A ***rógaire*** can refer to a "chancer," or someone who is willing to take advantage of people or situations for their own advantage. ***Rógaire*** is also used to describe those who exploit others for their own personal financial gain, like a fraudster or a hustler. Like many multifunctional words *as Gaeilge*, appropriate tone and delivery is required to get the correct message across, and ***rógaire*** is no exception.

seafóid | seafóideach NOUN | ADJECTIVE

(shaf-oh-idh) | *(shaf-oh-djuch)*

nonsense | nonsensical

An Irish speaker's vocabulary would simply be boring in the absence of the words ***seafóid*** and ***seafóideach***. ***Seafóid*** is used in the same ways as its many English counterparts such as "a load of nonsense" or "a load of garbage." If someone's telling you a story that just seems too far-fetched to be true, call their bluff with a "what a load of ***seafóid***!" Similarly, you could exclaim "*Tá sé sin* ***seafóideach***!" *(taw shay shin shaf-oh-djuch)*, meaning "That's ridiculous" or "That's nonsense!" Given that the letter *s* at the beginning of the word is followed by a slender vowel, the *s* is slender, meaning it's pronounced *(shhh)*. To add emphasis, the *(shhh)* sound at the beginning can really be dragged out.

Although ***seafóid*** and ***seafóideach*** aren't inherently curse words, using them gives off the same energy and disbelief as the word in English that can be shortened to b.s. ***Seafóid*** and ***seafóideach*** are like *Gaeilge* gold dust; they add immense character and rhythm to any conversation and interaction. They function as an energetic interjection that can be seamlessly thrown into the conversation even in an all-English environment. The delivery plays a large role in the understanding of these words. Even for someone who's never encountered *Gaeilge* in their life, they can easily understand what you mean by exclaiming "***seafóid!***" and "***seafóideach***," through context alone.

seanchaí | seanchas NOUN | NOUN

(shan-a-kee) | *(shan-a-kuss)*

storyteller | storytelling

Before the reign of TV, streaming services, podcasts, and modern media, there was the reign of the ***seanchaí***. While people now gather around screens for entertainment, the ***seanchaí*** was the center of attention and adoration at Irish gatherings for many centuries. In a literal sense, the word ***seanchaí*** means "the bearer of old lore," meaning that people bestowed with this illustrious title were viewed as historians and storytellers. In late medieval Ireland, the role of a ***seanchaí*** was highly respected by local chieftains and contemporary society, as they had a wide range of roles including dealing with literature, genealogy, and legal issues. However, from the 1500s onward, following the British conquests of Ireland, the role of the ***seanchaí*** became more centered on storytelling alone. As Ireland had one of the richest folklore traditions in the world, the ***seanchaí*** was entrusted as a custodian of spoken word, history, and mythology, and therefore, became the means of the preservation and sharing of oral literature. The historic practice of ***seanchas*** (storytelling) is still highly prevalent among Irish communities to this day, and Ireland has gained the reputation of captivating storytellers due to this pastime alone.

sean-nós NOUN

(SHAN-know-ss)

traditional Irish singing and dancing

The expression ***sean-nós*** literally translates to "old custom" or "traditional manner" and refers to a historic style of singing and dancing in Ireland. ***Sean-nós*** singing dates back centuries and is an unaccompanied vocal style renowned for melodic harmonies and glottal stops. Songs of this genre cover a wide variety of powerful themes, such as love, laments, grief, emigration, history, famine, and nature; they feature stylistic differences between regions. The tradition of ***sean-nós*** is a powerful storytelling tool that captivates audiences and connects both singers and listeners with emotions and authentic experiences. Songs were traditionally passed down orally for generations, preserving the Irish language as a whole. Given that the style is a cappella, it creates an engaging listening experience that invites audiences to connect with the evocative lyrics; singers will often close their eyes for the duration of the performance. Groups will gather, sit in a circle, and take turns to sing. Each performance will be intently listened to and respected. ***Sean-nós*** dancing is a solo style that is performed in a hard shoe similar to those worn for tap dancing. The dance was traditionally performed in informal settings, such as in social gatherings, at parties, or in pubs, and the steps are often improvised by the dancer. Although this style now features heavily as a category in competitions and organized cultural events, it is a more casual style than set dancing or *céilí* dancing.

seisiún NOUN

(se-shoon)

session; a musical or drinking gathering

The word ***seisiún*** or "session" is multifunctional in Irish culture. In a traditional and historical sense, a ***seisiún*** refers to either an impromptu or planned gathering of traditional Irish musicians, typically in a pub or house (similar to the concept of a *céilí*). In present day, a ***seisiún*** can be organized in local halls and community centers, as well as in Irish cultural and arts centers across the globe. These are referred to as a *seisiún ceoil as Gaeilge* (*ceoil* meaning "music") or a "trad session" in English; "trad" referring to traditional Irish music. If a group of traditional Irish musicians is confined or gathered in one space, you can be guaranteed that a ***seisiún*** will break out. These are lively affairs that follow no given structure or set list, and any musician in the vicinity is invited to join in. Given the casual nature of a *seisiún ceoil*, you will often find a group of musicians huddled in the corner of a pub playing away to their hearts content, as opposed to being onstage. A structured, preplanned performance contradicts the openness of an authentic *seisiún ceoil.* In terms of cultural modern-day slang, a "session" can refer to a general social gathering (typically with the intention of drinking) that is not centered around traditional Irish music. "Session" is commonly shortened to "sesh," and if one is "on the sesh" it means they are out and about, drinking.

Sheasfainn sa sneachta le héisteacht leat PHRASE

(HYAS-hinn sah SHNOK-tah leh HAYSH-tucht lyat)

I would stand in the snow to listen to you (declaration of love)

In case pickup lines like *Ar mhaith leat a bheith curtha le mo mhuintir*? (Would you like to be buried with my family?) aren't your cup of tea, here's another option that's more likely to pull at the heart strings. ***Sheasfainn sa sneachta le héisteacht leat*** literally translates to "I would stand in the snow to listen to you." This one is actually romantic. In confessing this expression to someone, you are conveying that you are willing to brave the elements just to hear the sound of their beautiful voice, regardless of what they have to say. As either a declaration of love or a pickup line, one could rightfully be quite hopeful of its prospective success rate.

Sheasfainn is the conditional tense conjugation of the verb *seas* (meaning "to stand"), *sa sneachta* means "in the snow," and finally *le héisteacht leat* is "to listen to you." In the Irish language, one doesn't listen *to* something, but instead one listens *with* someone. Hence why the prepositional pronoun *leat*, meaning "with you," is used in this phrase instead of *duit* meaning "to you." "I'd Stand in the Snow" is a 2017 song by Charlie McGettigan, Irish singer, songwriter, and Eurovision winner, who was inspired by this phrase.

Sláinte chuig na fir 's go mairfidh na mná go deo PHRASE

(slawin-cha chwig na fihr iss guh MAR-ee nah m-naw guh joe)

Health to the men and may the women live forever

By this point, you should have quite the repertoire of toasts *as Gaeilge* built up and **Sláinte chuig na fir 's go mairfidh na mná go deo** is no exception. This is a toast that is typically delivered in two parts and requires both cooperation and concentration. The men will toast themselves first and they deliver the first section of the phrase: *sláinte chuig na fir*, meaning "health to the men." Irish women couldn't let the men have the upper hand; therefore, they gave themselves a stronger toast. The second section of this toast, *'s go mairfidh na mná go deo*, means "and may the women live forever." So, the men wish health upon themselves, but the women wish eternal health upon themselves. The women ultimately have the upper hand.

Straight Home after Mass In 1878, the Sunday Closure Act was passed in Ireland, which reduced pubs' trading hours on a Sunday to 2 p.m. until 7 p.m. This was in an effort to encourage men and husbands to return to their wives and children after Sunday morning mass instead of going straight to the pub. Some cities with a population of over five thousand, however, were granted longer opening hours until 9 p.m. After the enactment of the Sunday Closure Act, arrests for drunkenness fell 53 percent.

uisce beatha | fuisce NOUN

(ishka BAH-hah) | *(fwishka)*

whiskey

Scotch this, bourbon that; time to talk about whiskey. The word "whiskey" itself comes from the Irish-language word ***fuisce***, which was later anglicized to "whiskey." The term ***uisce beatha*** is also used for this beverage, and it yields a deeper literal translation. *Uisce* is the word *as Gaeilge* for "water" and *beatha* refers to "life." Therefore, ***uisce beatha*** literally translates to "the water of life." This translation can be linked to the Latin term *aqua vitae*, also meaning "water of life," which was first used by the Bishop of Ossory, Richard de Ledrede in 1324 when he documented his recipe to refer to a strong alcoholic distilled beverage. The origination of this grain distilled spirit in Ireland dates back to roughly the twelfth century, meaning it is one of the earliest distilled beverages in Europe; however, the Scots and the Irish debate who was the first to produce the beverage.

To tell the difference between the Irish and Scottish drink, one must pay attention to the spelling; "whisky" (with no e) refers to the Scottish drink whereas "whiskey" (with an e) refers to the Irish drink. Irish whiskey has gained global popularity, but it has faced some challenges on its journey to notoriety. In 1556, English Parliament passed an act so that the production of ***uisce beatha*** was illegal without a license. So, the drink was distilled largely in secret and away from the east coast of the country, where British rule was most palpable.

5 Rituals and Traditions

There is no shortage of quirky and equally beautiful rituals and traditions on the Emerald Isle. These customs have been carried by the Irish people to every corner of the world and have an innate beauty and cultural magnitude that enamors the masses. As a nation, the Irish are immensely proud of their rituals and traditions that have been protected, preserved, and cultivated by past generations. To understand Irish practices is to connect with an ancient civilization: the Celts. These traditions hail from a people who inhabited Ireland centuries ago; that they are still practiced to this day is a truly beautiful phenomenon and serves as proof of the resilience and cultural integrity of the Irish.

an fáinne NOUN

(on FAWN-yah)

the ring (a badge)

An fáinne, which translates to "the ring," is a brooch worn on one's lapel and serves as an identifier to those around you that you are a speaker of the Irish language. In wearing a *fáinne* you are not only expressing that you are an Irish speaker, but that you wish for others to also speak the language with you. ***An fáinne*** is an important symbol within the Irish-speaking community that allows speakers to easily identify each other; it ensures that the wearers of this ring do not miss out on opportunities to converse through the Irish language. There are variations of ***an fáinne*** that align with one's level of fluency. A golden *fáinne* is worn by those who are native speakers or fully fluent. A silver *fáinne* signifies an Irish speaker of intermediate level, or someone who has a functional level of the language—enough to engage in conversation. Finally, a copper or bronze *fáinne* is worn by those who may possess *cúpla focal*, "a few words" of Irish or no Irish at all but are interested in the language and want to learn more. This system allows Irish speakers to conduct conversations with an understanding of the other's level of fluency.

Bealtaine NOUN

(BYAL-thin-eh)

Celtic festival in May

Bealtaine is the third Celtic festival of the Gregorian calendar and the penultimate of the pagan calendar. Celebrated on May 1, this festival marked the arrival of the summer months and weather suitable for crop growth. In ancient Ireland, houses and even livestock would be decorated with yellow May flowers and people often visited holy wells, praying for a bountiful summer. The pagans believed the *sióg*, "fairies," of the otherworld to be especially active during this season, and therefore people would take ***Bealtaine*** as an opportunity to make offerings to these mythological beings as to keep the peace. On the morning of May 1, women would wash their faces with the dew gathered from the grass, because people believed you would remain beautiful the entire year as the dew washed away the mask hiding your inner beauty. According to legend, the dew gathered on petals and the grass of ***Bealtaine*** is charged with the energy of the otherworld and possesses the energy of rebirth and blossoming beauty, a core value of the festival itself. ***Bealtaine*** is a magnificent festival that provides people with the opportunity to connect with the beauty of nature and celebrate warmth and light coming into the brighter summer months; it's a special time appreciated by the ancient pagans and people across the globe.

cáca baile NOUN

(KAW-kah BAL-eh)

soda bread

Cáca baile, or Irish soda bread, is a staple in Irish households. *Cáca* means "cake," or in this case "loaf," and *baile* means "home," meaning that ***cáca baile*** literally translates to "home-made cake" or "local cake." In Irish English, ***cáca baile*** is most commonly referred to as "soda bread," which stems from the 1830s when baking soda was first introduced to Ireland. The Native Americans are the first known to use baking soda to rise their bread without yeast. A cross would be scored into the surface of the ***cáca baile*** dough—not for aesthetic purposes, but as a superstitious practice. They did this because it was believed to release the fairies, or *sióg* (because who wants to eat fairy-infested bread), and to ward off evil and protect the household. The baking of ***cáca baile*** plays a significant role in Irish culture and identity and is an integral element of many Irish homes.

Churching "Churching" was a ritual performed by the Irish Catholic Church whereby new mothers would receive a blessing four to six weeks after giving birth in thanks for a safe delivery. This ritual was also referred to as "The Purification of Women" and mothers would be prohibited from certain activities, like baking bread, until they had been "churched." Given that the woman was seen as "unpure" until she received this special blessing, the bread baked by her would subsequently not be fit for consumption.

caoineadh VERB

(kween-eh)

keening; to lament the dead

Don't let it be said that the Celts weren't resourceful—they used to outsource their mourning. ***Caoineadh*** is a form of *sean-nós* singing performed by professional female mourners at funerals throughout Ireland, Scotland, and the Isle of Man. First recorded in the twelfth century, this tradition was described as a ritualistic funeral song to emphasize the feelings of grief and loss felt by the departed's loved ones. A woman would walk in a circle around the body of the deceased while singing, or "keening," and fellow mourners would join in by rocking back and forth to the rhythm of the ***caoineadh***. This practice began to die out in the seventeenth century when the Catholic Church threatened excommunication to those who practiced this tradition, which they deemed pagan.

Banshee, or *Bean Sí*? In modern days, the "banshee" is depicted as a frightening, wailing harbinger of death, but this mythical creature stems from Irish folklore and mythology and the Celtic tradition of ***caoineadh***. The modern word "banshee" stems from the Irish *bean sí (ban she)*. The anglicization of the spelling and pronunciation certainly didn't push the boat out too much in this case. A combination of the tradition of ***caoineadh*** and the Irish mythological creature, the *bean sí*, results in the modern-day depiction of the "banshee."

cleamhnas NOUN

(CLOWN-iss)

matchmaking

The art of ***cleamhnas***, "matchmaking," has had a large and special role in Irish society for many centuries. This tradition finds its roots in an era of Irish history when courting, and finding oneself a partner, was of significant societal importance. Matchmakers themselves were known as *fear cleamhnais (far clyown-ish)*, translating to "man of matchmaking," and they would be the organizers of matchmaking events. Traditionally, this role would fall to the parish priest, but in the twentieth-century modernization of dating, the role of the matchmaker would be given to the most extroverted married man of the parish. The *fear cleamhnais* would meet with families in advance of the festival to negotiate dowries, land, and wealth transfers, as well as other marital affairs. If, at the end of the festival, all parties involved were content with the match, a formal agreement, essentially a marital contract, was drawn up for the new couple.

Lisdoonvarna Matchmaking Festival Lisdoonvarna, in County Clare, is renowned for its annual matchmaking festival, the largest of its kind in Europe. Taking place in September, the festival attracts over sixty thousand hopeful singletons. This festival is so iconic that a movie was made about it in 1997. *The Matchmaker* features a US senator's assistant who is sent to Ireland to hunt down Irish relatives and finds herself in a Matchmaking Festival.

cloch na Blarnan NOUN

(kluck nah BLAHR-nan)

Blarney Stone

Housed within Blarney Castle, ***cloch na Blarnan*** is one of the most famous and world-renowned tourist attractions in Ireland. Legend has it, if you kiss "the Blarney Stone," you're given the gift of eloquence and the skill of flattery. More commonly referred to as "the gift of the gab," this is a skill that many Irish people possess. As to where the Blarney Stone garnered this power, there is no definitive answer. The truth has been lost to time and the story has grown through the Irish people's innate ability to weave a good story.

The most plausible explanation as to the powers of ***cloch na Blarnan*** involves Queen Elizabeth I and a man named Cormac Teige McCarthy. Queen Elizabeth I wanted Irish chiefs to occupy their own land under titles from the Queen herself. The Lord of Blarney, Cormac Teige McCarthy himself, then commandeered his Irish wit to satisfy the Queen and forgo having to sign over his rights and titles of his land. In thanks, he kissed ***cloch na Blarnan*** and bestowed his wit upon it. Far-fetched? Perhaps, but who's going to question the "gift of the gab."

cneasaí NOUN

(ku-NAHS-ee)

healer

A ***cneasaí*** is a "healer" and a member of society who was highly respected and valued historically in Ireland and still is to this day in modern culture. Through word of mouth, strange tales, practices, and concoctions, the ancient Celts devised many cures for healing both physical and mental ailments for over 2,500 years. These historic healing traditions are embedded in Irish culture. "The cure" refers to the ***cneasaí***'s innate healing ability, as opposed to referring to the treatment itself. Therefore, you will often hear Irish people saying that so and so has "the cure" for a particular ailment, meaning that they possess the said "cure" and the ability to perform it.

Deep-rooted in the Irish oral tradition, finding a ***cneasaí*** is accomplished through word of mouth. Advertising oneself as a healer or accepting payment for administering "the cure" is highly frowned upon. A very common example of a belief-based cure is that the seventh son of a seventh son will inherit the ability to cure an ailment. Although "the cure" itself might sound wacky, Irish people know not to question the ***cneasaí***. Some examples include licking a burn, blessing a stye with your mother's gold wedding ring, sheep's droppings boiled in milk to cure whooping cough, and more. Note that "the cure" in this case is not the same as the alcohol-related "cure" mentioned in Chapter 4.

Cruach Phádraig NOUN

(CREW-uch PHAW-drig)

Croagh Patrick

Cruach Phádraig in County Mayo is a mountain that stands 764 meters (2,507 feet) tall and is described as the holiest mountain in Ireland. This is one of Ireland's many Christian pilgrimage sites and its ties to religion go back thousands of years. The mystical origins of the mountain are pagan, with archaeologists having found remnants and artifacts of pagan Celtic worship from the Neolithic (New Stone Age) period. Evidence suggests that ***Cruach Phádraig*** was used as a massive bonfire beacon for the festival of *Lúnasa*, marking the beginning of the harvest season.

This mountain is named after Ireland's patron saint, St. Patrick, as it's said that he climbed to the mountain's summit around C.E. 441 to fast for forty days and forty nights, imitating the Lord's pilgrimage to the desert. Many will climb the mountain with a specific wish, goal, or intention in mind, like to wish good health upon their loved ones, but it is believed that you must climb the mountain three times to receive your wish. Those who are particularly daring, or those who have much to atone for, will climb the mountain barefoot to show true humility, penance, and devotion.

Éire go brách PHRASE

(AIR-ah guh BRAW-kh)

Ireland forever; Ireland until doomsday

The phrase ***Éire go brách*** is the epitome of Irish patriotism. Encapsulating a deep, intense love for Ireland, this phrase translates to "Ireland forever," "Ireland until doomsday," or "Ireland until judgment day." Unfortunately, like other phrases in Irish, anglicized versions of ***Éire go brách*** have become widely recognized. This anglicization can be seen as "Erin go bragh" or sometimes "Erin go braugh." Be aware of the anglicizations and subsequently avoid them, because anglicization is not your friend, nor should you add to its use any further. ***Éire go brách*** is seen adorned on items such as tote bags and sweatshirts as a demonstration of one's loyalty to Ireland and wish for the country's longevity and prosperity. Using this phrase exemplifies a love for not only the country of Ireland but all that she entails: language, culture, traditions, and history.

Éire | Éirinn | Éireann A point of confusion for many Irish language learners is the variations in spelling seen when referring to the country of Ireland *as Gaeilge*, but the answer is quite simple. *Éire* is the nominative form when simply naming the country. For example, *Is breá liom Éire*, meaning "I love Ireland." *Éirinn* is used after prepositions. For example, *Táim i mo chónaí in Éirinn*, meaning "I live in Ireland." Finally, *Éireann* is the genitive form implemented in many cases, one of which being to express possession. For example, *muintir na hÉireann*, meaning "the people of Ireland."

fáinne Chladaigh NOUN

(fawn-yah chlah-dig)

Claddagh ring

The ***fáinne Chladaigh*** is a ring that may symbolize love, friendship, or loyalty in Irish culture. This jewelry has gained a notable rise in popularity recently due to the Irish culture appreciation movement. The crown of the design symbolizes loyalty, the heart symbolizes love, and the clasped hands symbolize friendship. The ***fáinne Chladaigh*** reportedly hails from Claddagh in County Galway and was designed by local goldsmith Richard Joyce in the seventeenth century.

The interesting thing about the ***fáinne Chladaigh*** is how one chooses to wear it. When single, the ring is worn on the fourth digit of the right hand with the heart facing away from the body. When in a relationship, the ring is turned around so that the heart faces you, signifying that your heart is closed. When engaged, the ring is worn on the ring finger with the heart facing out and finally, when married, the ring is turned around with the heart facing in.

Cut the Crown An alternate style of ***fáinne Chladaigh*** is the Fenian Claddagh. This style features the traditional embraced hands and heart of the Claddagh ring, but the crown is removed (as some believe it's tied to the monarchy and British colonialism). This style emerged in the nineteenth century, when Irish nationalists were seeking independence from British rule. Some people would break off this part of the ring's design, so jewelers offer crownless rings.

fidchell NOUN

(fi-chell)

Celtic chess

Fidchell, literally translating to "wisdom of the wood," is often referred to as Celtic chess. It's centuries older than today's chess (which is called *ficheall* in modern Irish). An excavation performed in 1932 revealed a ***fidchell*** board that was dated to C.E. 950–975. ***Fidchell*** is a two-person game and was predominantly played by the elites of ancient Celtic societies: kings, queens, knights, and druids. The premise of the game surrounded either attacking or defending the High King of Ireland. One player, the defender, would have eight pieces, two per province. The attacker would have twelve pieces, three per province. The game was played on a plane of forty-nine squares.

Not only was ***fidchell*** an opportunity to demonstrate one's skill to their opposition, but the tradition served as entertainment to a live audience as well. The skill, strategy, and fierce competitiveness displayed by ***fidchell*** players wasn't the only focus of the game, however. ***Fidchell*** would also be used ceremonially in Celtic societies to forecast and predict prophesies from the pagan gods. The tradition of ***fidchell***, like many ancient Irish practices, has been preserved and is enjoyed by both young and old to this day. So, next time you find yourself playing a game of chess, pay tribute to the Celts and say you're playing a game of *ficheall.*

geansaí Árann NOUN

(gyan-ZEE aw-RINN)

Aran jumper (sweater)

To visit Ireland without making the scenic voyage to visit the Aran Islands on the west coast is a mortal sin. An even bigger sin than that would be to return to the mainland without a ***geansaí Árann***, an "Aran jumper." ("Jumper" is another word for "sweater"—the only one Irish people use.) The ***geansaí Árann*** has become a foolproof way of identifying tourists in Ireland, but these jumpers kept islanders warm and protected from the harsh Atlantic coast elements for hundreds of years.

The ***geansaí Árann*** would have been traditionally hand-knit by the local women of the Aran Islands using the wool of sheep or goats. This material has a water-resistant nature, which is advantageous when facing the rainy conditions of the west coast—an area of Ireland where it rains for an average of over 230 days a year. Although the ***geansaí Árann*** is a practical item of clothing due to its warmth and water-resistant nature, it also serves as a prime example of beautiful Irish craftsmanship. Intricate patterns are woven throughout the jumpers to represent traditional familial patterns, similar to the tartans of kilts in Scotland. Tragically, however, another reason why families had distinctive patterns knitted onto their jumpers was to identify the bodies of fishermen lost at sea and later washed ashore.

Imbolc NOUN

(ihm-BULL-uk)

Cross quarter day; pagan festival

Imbolc is the first Celtic festival in the Gregorian calendar and celebrated on February 1. To mark the end of winter, plants, crops, and flowers were planted by the greater clan as a whole. Candles and torches were lit to symbolize the returning of the sun and the return of longer daylight hours. An altar was created to give offerings and thanks to the goddess Brigid, the goddess of spring, fertility, and life. In ancient times, the altar was constructed on top of a stone dolmen in the outdoors, in nature. However, if you wish to celebrate ***Imbolc*** in the twenty-first century, an indoor altar on a table would suffice.

When Christianity became the dominant Irish belief, elements of paganism were incorporated into the celebration of Christian holidays. New days of worship were created to include the customs and traditions of the Irish. For example, St. Brigid became the new Christian saint and symbol of spring for the Irish. Her feast day is also celebrated on February 1.

Spring Clean, or *Imbolc* Clean? **If you have ever conducted a spring clean, you have already celebrated *Imbolc*. During *Imbolc* celebrations, items deemed unnecessary from the previous year were discarded, and both the household and village were cleaned up, symbolizing a fresh start for the season. The origins of a spring clean can be linked to paganism, Jewish Passover traditions, and the Persian new year, Nowruz.**

Lá an Dreoilín NOUN

(law on droel-een)

Wren Day

Lá an Dreoilín, The Wren Day, is celebrated on December 26 and is also known as St. Stephen's Day in Ireland, or Boxing Day in England. Traditionally, groups of Irish men and boys would hunt and kill the wren bird, giving the practice its name. *An dreoilín* is "the wren" and is regarded as the king of birds in Ireland because it was seen as the messenger of the Celtic gods. Therefore, hunting and killing this creature constituted great notoriety and was only allowed on this one day of the year.

While the tradition of hunting *an dreoilín* on ***Lá an Dreoilín*** is long gone, this special day survives in a new format, particularly in western Ireland. People drape themselves in straw costumes and sing through the streets of their local town. These performers are called "wren boys" and lookers-on give money to them, which is used for charity or to upgrade and improve local amenities.

The Irish Macarena "*An Dreoilín*" is a song and dance among Irish speakers, garnering the same level of enthusiasm and group morale as the "Macarena." Although the lyrics of the song itself are quite gruesome as they depict the *dreoilín* getting eaten by a cat, this dance is taught to children and is performed at gatherings such as a *céilí*. The dance varies depending on the region but is largely simple and repetitive, and it follows the same structure as the "Macarena" whereby a sequence of moves is completed and all those participating then make a ninety-degree turn in unison.

Lá Fhéile Bríde NOUN

(law EYL-eh BREEDj-eh)

St. Brigid's Day

Lá Fhéile Bríde (St. Brigid's Day) is February 1 and is an opportunity to celebrate Ireland's only patroness: Saint Brigid. The most popular way of celebrating ***Lá Fhéile Bríde***, both historically and today, is to craft a St. Brigid's cross. This is a cross or crucifix that is weaved with rush reeds. These reeds are found generally growing wildly and bountifully in the wet fields of Ireland after a long, harsh winter. However, if you can't access the reeds and still want to craft a St. Brigid's cross, you can use straw, hay, quills, thin strips of paper, pipe cleaners, twine, string, or any other available material. The opportunities are endless. A St. Brigid's cross is traditionally placed above the door of the household, or above the fireplace. It is also custom to leave a piece of cloth or ribbon outside of the front door of your house on the eve of ***Lá Fhéile Bríde***, which is said to grant safe passage to travelers.

Bountiful Brigids There are just about as many variations of the name Brigid in Ireland as there are actual people with the name. Brigid, Brighid, Bridget, Brid, Bríd, Breda, Brida . . . the list goes on. The number of baby girls with this name peaked in the year 1965 with 293 Brigids being born. Although this name has recently declined in popularity, the spirit of Brigid lives on.

Lá Fhéile Pádraig NOUN

(law EYL-eh PAW-drig)

St. Patrick's Day

Every March 17, millions worldwide adorn themselves in green to celebrate ***Lá Fhéile Pádraig***, or St. Patrick's Day. ***Lá Fhéile Pádraig*** has two names in the English language. If you want to be more formal, feel free to elect for the full "Saint Patrick's Day." Informally in Ireland, the name of this festival is abbreviated to "Saint Paddy's Day" (*not* "Saint Patty's Day"). As per the Irish language, *Pádraig* is the name "Patrick," which gave rise to the extremely common name in Ireland, "Paddy." Note the letter *d* in "Paddy," as it stems from *Pádraig*. Saying "Saint Patty's Day" is sure to rub Irish people the wrong way, as the double letter *t* emerged from an alteration of "Patrick," as opposed to *Pádraig*. ***Lá Fhéile Pádraig*** is a time of immense patriotism for Irish people and certainly a time to avoid anglicization.

St. Patrick Isn't Just for the Irish Arguably, Ireland is most renowned for its patron saint Patrick, and his feast day, but Ireland is not the only country that can claim him. Saint Patrick was named the patron saint of Nigeria in 1961 when Ireland opened its embassy in Lagos. The ties between Ireland and Nigeria don't stop there: Guinness is the second most popular beer in the country and is brewed locally with maize, instead of European barley.

Lúnasa NOUN

(loo-nih-sah)

Celtic festival marking the beginning of the harvest season

Lúnasa is an ancient Celtic festival celebrated on August 1 to mark the transition from autumn to winter; it's named after the pagan god *Lugh*. *Lugh* is a complex god associated with light, skill, craftsmanship, war, justice, and sovereignty. The festival of ***Lúnasa*** sits upon three core value pillars: abundance, renewal, and community. This festival is a celebration of the harvest; communities would gather to celebrate a (hopefully) bountiful harvest and the store of crops crucial to survive the winter months. Pagans expressed their gratitude to the fertility of the earth, reflecting on the cycle of life, death, and rebirth. They lit bonfires on this special day, just like the other pagan festivals, but these were not as central to the celebration as for the others. ***Lúnasa*** is also a time for sports and competitions; according to folklore, it is believed that *Lugh* initially organized the festival as a sporting occasion.

Celtic Olympics The *Tailteann (tahl-tihn)* Games were basically the Celtic Olympic Games. There is a historic divide between the ancient and modern *Tailteann* Games as they were re-established in 1924 through 1932. These games were held in County Meath from 632 B.C.E. until C.E. 1168 and combined aspects of traditional sports, song, poetry, dancing, and music. The ancient *Tailteann* Games started about one hundred forty years after the ancient Olympic Games but lasted almost eight hundred years longer.

Naomh Antaine NOUN

(NAY-v ahn-TIN-ah)

St. Anthony

Although ***Naomh Antaine***, or St. Anthony, can't wholly be claimed by the Irish, he certainly holds a special and highly respected place in the hearts of the nation. He is referred to almost exclusively as "Holy Saint Anthony" in Ireland. This is peculiar as no other saint, even the patron saints Patrick and Brigid, receive the same exclamation of "Holy" before their title. ***Naomh Antaine*** is whom you may turn to when an item has been lost or misplaced. An example of a prayer used in these instances is "Holy Saint Anthony: Look around, find something that can't be found." It is commonly observed that nine times out of ten upon praying to ***Naomh Antaine***, he pulls through and the item you have been searching for will seemingly magically appear. Whether this is down to coincidence or faith is unknown, but the phenomenon is not to be questioned. When you have called upon ***Naomh Antaine*** and he has come to your aid, it is customary to donate money to the ***Naomh Antaine*** charity collection boxes that can be found in shops and pubs. Throwing a few coins into these boxes or "giving a copper to Holy St. Anthony" expresses your thanks for his assistance and ensures that he will help again.

Nollaig na mBan NOUN

(nuh-LIG nah mawn)

Women's Christmas

Nollaig na mBan is now regarded as a celebration of womanhood, but the practice began as a means of appreciating the women in your family. This Irish Christmas tradition should be shared with, loved, and adopted by the world. On January 6, people stop to appreciate women and their hard work in creating festive magic over the Christmas period. Traditionally, roles would be reversed on this day, and men would take over childcare and housework to give the women a well-deserved day off. Women would visit each other's homes to catch up and relax over a cup of tea while indulging on the last of the Christmas treats. However, given that January 6 is officially the twelfth and last day of Christmas, some thought it hypocritical that the women were left with the remaining scraps on ***Nollaig na mBan*** in comparison to the feasts served on Christmas Day itself. Today, the tradition of women coming together to celebrate ***Nollaig na mBan*** is still very strong and shares the same sentiment as Galentine's Day.

January 6 isn't a date *only* reserved for ***Nollaig na mBan***, however, as this is a significant date in the broader Christian belief. The sixth day of January, also referred to as "Epiphany" or "Little Christmas," celebrates the arrival of the Three Wise Men bringing gifts, and Christian cultures around the world have various customs and rituals performed on this date.

Oíche Shamhna NOUN

(ee-ha HOW-nah)

Halloween

You can thank the Irish (or Celts) for spooky season. That's right, Halloween stems from a pagan festival. ***Oíche Shamhna***, or *Samhain (Sow-in)*, was celebrated on November 1 and was the division between the brighter summer months and the cold, dark winter months; it's like the Celtic equivalent of New Year's Eve. The Celts believed the veil between the living and the dead realms was its thinnest during this time of year. Rituals were performed to ward off evil and protect one's clan, livestock, and crops. Plus, bonfires would be lit, and people would adorn themselves in revolting costumes to scare off spirits. Although the community was often on-edge during *Samhain*, families gathered around the bonfire for warmth and took embers to relight their own hearth's fires. ***Oíche Shamhna*** traditions and practices were carried by the Irish people to America during the mass emigration of the 1800s.

Carve a Turnip Irish people historically carved scary faces into turnips on ***Oíche Shamhna*** to ward off evil spirits like Stingy Jack. Stingy Jack was a man who tricked the devil, thus denying himself entry to both heaven and hell, and ultimately sentencing himself to roam the earth forever. In carving a ghostly face into a turnip and illuminating the ghoulish grin with a flame, the Irish hoped to scare off Stingy Jack. This tradition gives life to what is now the infamous "jack-o'-lantern," carved from America's populous pumpkin crop.

piseog | piseoga NOUN

(pish-OHG) | (pish-ohg-ah)

superstition(s)

The Irish are extremely superstitious, a sentiment believed to stem from ancient Celtic folklore, traditions, and customs. However, some believe that the superstitious nature of the Irish can be attributed to the age of their culture, and therefore they possess a naturally intuitive way of thinking. However, many of the inherently Irish ***piseoga***, or superstitions, can also be tied to the strong presence of the Catholic church in Ireland. In many instances, the ***piseoga*** observed by the Irish can seem wacky and wonderful, but they can usually be justified by ancient customs or traditions.

Piseoga have been spread across Ireland by word of mouth and have also been passed down from generation to generation. Although the younger generations of the Irish may not be as intrinsically superstitious as their ancestors, these practices are largely respected and adhered to by the majority. Though you may try to reason with yourself that nothing bad will *actually* happen if you don't abide by the ***piseoga***, many a tale has been shared of those who suffered the wrath of doing so. These tales and beliefs are so engrained in the Irish that they feel it best not to tempt fate.

Síle na gCíoch NOUN

(SHEEL-ah nah GEE-ockh)

Sheela na Gig

If you don't know who ***Síle na gCíoch*** is, soon you'll know. The anglicized spelling of this feminist icon's name, "Sheela na Gig," is widely used, but this book is sticking with either ***Síle na Gig*** or ***Síle na gCíoch*** for obvious authenticity reasons. ***Síle na Gig*** presents herself as a stone carving of a female figure with an exaggerated vulva, often using her two hands to pull it open. These carvings can be seen, unexpectedly, in churches, and in castles and other stone buildings across both the island of Ireland and other parts of continental Europe. The oldest carvings of ***Síle na Gig*** date back to the eleventh century, making her medieval in nature and a feature of Romanesque church art.

There are many believed interpretations of her symbolism; for example, the belief that ***Síle na Gig*** is a representation of Celtic goddesses or older pagan symbolism of the sacred feminine and fertility. However, in a Christian context, ***Síle na Gig*** could have been viewed as a representation of the sin of lust, and she served as a warning against sexual temptation. In modern times, the effigy of ***Síle na Gig*** fulfills female empowerment and feminist reinterpretation. She can be seen bountifully in modern art, adorned on T-shirts, stickers, tote bags, and so on. Therefore, ***Síle na Gig*** is a perfect example of how historic traditions are being appreciated and carried into the twenty-first century by modern Gaelic communities.

siόg NOUN

(she-oge)

fairy

Irish fairies (**sióg**) are supernatural beings deeply embedded in Irish mythology and folklore. **Sióg** reside in "the Otherworld," a mystical realm that exists alongside, beneath, above, and within this one. The entrance to the Otherworld is marked by fairy trees and fairy forts (circular earthen mounds). If either are interfered with, you'll provoke the wrath of the fairies.

Although the word "fairy" may create a mental image of a cute, innocent being with wings and a magical wand, in Irish folklore, the fairy folk are not to be messed with. **Sióg** are highly respected in Irish culture, but they're regarded with fear. Hanging a garland of marigolds and primroses above your door; wearing a bag of ash, rowan, and blackthorn wood around your neck; and turning your coat inside out are all superstitious practices meant to protect you from the mischievous **sióg**.

Make Way for Fairies The Irish belief in sióg is so intense that the construction of the M18 motorway between Galway and Limerick was delayed for over ten years because the proposed route would have required the demolition of a fairy bush. A renowned local *seanchaí* (storyteller) fought for the preservation of the fairy bush as he urged that its destruction would massively unsettle the fairy folk and lead to deaths on the motorway. Long story short, the M18 was rerouted, and the fairy bush still stands to this day.

snag breac NOUN

(snawg brack)

magpie

In Irish folklore, the ***snag breac***, the magpie, is heavily associated with superstition and good or bad omen. Whether the ***snag breac*** brings good or bad tidings is dependent on the quantity in which they appear to the beholder and is conveniently laid out in this rhyme: "One for sorrow, two for joy, three for a girl, four for a boy, five for silver, six for gold, seven for a secret never to be told." An older and slightly more sinister version of the rhyme first recorded in 1777 reads, "One for sorrow, two for joy, three for a funeral, four for birth, five for heaven, six for hell, seven for the devil, his own self." This begs the question of whether the rhyme was rebranded to have a lighter sentiment, or to make it actually rhyme. Regardless, it is abundantly clear that as per folklore and superstition, seeing a single ***snag breac*** on its own is a bad omen. Therefore, it is custom to salute or wave to a ***snag breac*** if you see one alone, as to make acquaintance in the hopes that it doesn't bring sorrow upon you. So, if you see an Irish person waving or saluting to what seems like thin air, assume that they are simply trying to avoid the wrath of the ***snag breac***.

snaidhm seirce NOUN

(sneem SHIRK-ah)

love knot

The expression "tying the knot" is a commonly used euphemism for getting married; it finds its origins in ancient Celtic knotwork. This practice of tapestry, intricate designs, and profound symbolism has woven (pun intended) its way into the fabric of countless cultures. These knots, formed by interwoven ropes, primarily represent the concept of eternity. However, there are eight types of Celtic knots, and each holds a different meaning.

The ***snaidhm seirce*** is the most renowned of the Celtic knots and translates to a "true-love knot." This style of knot is an integral aspect of the Irish and Scottish wedding tradition of "handfasting" whereby the couple will tie a ***snaidhm seirce*** into a rope during their wedding ceremony. An additional knot is added to the rope to represent any children that the couple may have, symbolizing growing unity and strength within the family. It's said that if a couple ties one to a tree and it holds for a year, their love will last forever.

The Not-So-Happy Couple Handfasting and the tying of a ***snaidhm seirce*** are some of the more romantic, symbolic wedding traditions within Irish culture. However, in some rural areas of Ireland, it is tradition for the wedding couple to be "kidnapped" by their loved ones, tied to a trailer, and pelted with anything from rotten eggs to fish guts. The couple is then paraded around their village.

snaois NOUN

(sneesh)

snuff

Snaois is a grounded, powdered tobacco that is inhaled through the nose. Originally cultivated in South America, tobacco was shipped worldwide by the Spanish and eventually was introduced to Ireland in 1548 by Sir Walter Raleigh, who planted the crop in his estate in Youghal, County Cork. "Snuff" was used as an easy, reliable, and fast-acting stimulant, allowing you to perk up after a long day's work or to stay up late at night reading, writing, and studying. In Ireland, ***snaois*** became popular in the eighteenth and nineteenth centuries where it was one of the few unifiers of working classes and aristocracy alike. One of the uniquely Irish uses for ***snaois*** was that it was heavily consumed during wakes (traditional Irish burial rituals). This was not only for its stimulating effects but also to lighten the mood and to cover the odor of the deceased. ***Snaois*** boxes became common fashion accessories across Ireland, and partaking in ***snaois*** sniffing was a common and cheap form of social interaction. This practice began to decline in popularity in the twentieth century when other forms of tobacco consumption (cigarettes and cigars) became more fashionable, easily available, and cheaper.

sochraid NOUN

(suckh-RIDJ)

funeral

A ***sochraid***, an Irish funeral, has been described as being more fun than a British wedding. As a nation, the Irish have a long history of embracing death and don't shy away from talking about grief and bereavement. A ***sochraid*** celebrates the life of the deceased, and there are strong customs and rituals carried out at Irish funerals and during the period of mourning to honor the departed. Although many of these practices may not be implemented to the same extent now, they are passed down from generation to generation and largely respected within the country. Traditionally, clocks were stopped in the home at the time of death as a mark of respect but also to prevent bad luck. Mirrors in the home or hospital where one had passed were covered to ensure the soul could pass on freely. Similarly, all windows and doors were opened to allow the spirit to move on. Standing between the deceased and the windows or doors is seen as blocking the spirit's exit and results in you being cursed.

The Sandwiches! There are few customs in Ireland more powerful than the tray of sandwiches. Whether it's a funeral or a fundraiser, if a community is gathering, plates of sandwiches will arrive in droves. For Irish women, and mothers in particular, the mention of a communal gathering results in quick work and plates of finger food. The sheer quantity of sandwiches at events is almost comical.

tine chnámh NOUN

(tih-nah CHNAW-v)

bonfire

Although fire has always been crucial to human survival and something that no one society can claim ownership over, you have the ancient Celts to thank for the word "bonfire" itself. In *Gaeilge*, ***tine chnámh*** literally translates to "bone fire." It's easy to see how the term resulted in "bonfire" over time.

The ***tine chnámh*** was integral to ancient Irish life as nearly every holiday, traditional event, and occasion would have a bonfire lit to mark the occasion. Bones were burned within most bonfires, as the Celts believed that in burning the bones of the animals from which they feasted, they were saying thanks to the gods for granting them a large bounty. Then of course there was the practical reason for using bones in a ***tine chnámh***: fuel. Though not known for being a great tinder, bones once alight stay burning for a long time.

Oíche Shin Seáin **Pronounced *(ee-hah hin shawn)*, this festival celebrated on June 23 keeps the Irish bonfire tradition alive. *Oíche Shin Seáin* served as a celebration of the middle of summer as it falls just two days after the summer solstice (June 21). Although the lighting of fires in Ireland is illegal, this festival is protected as a cultural practice. The fire symbolizes power and light. The smoke of the fire is believed to protect from diseases, and young women jumped through the flames to bring fertility and swift marriage upon themselves.**

tórramh NOUN

(THOER-ah)

wake; a vigil for the dead

The ***tórramh*** is a unique ritual of death that is more like a social gathering. At a ***tórramh***, the deceased is "waked" or laid out in their home, traditionally in their bed but, in modern days, in the coffin. Loved ones, relatives, and neighbors will visit to pay their respects, share fond memories, drink, sing, and play music. In the past, the deceased was kept in the home for two to three days before being placed in the coffin for the formal funeral proceedings because of alcohol. *Poitín* (a type of alcohol), when consumed in vast quantities, could comatose a person for days at a time. This led to instances where one would be pronounced dead, placed in the coffin, but then "wake" up (get it?) days later and find themself buried alive. Funerals were delayed, just in case.

The American Wake A ***tórramh*** was not only held for the dead, but also for the living. The "American Wake" was a tradition that originated in the 1800s in Ireland, a time when vast numbers of Irish emigrants left behind a life of poverty in Ireland in hopes of prosperous new beginnings in the States. At this time, moving to America meant slim chances of seeing your loved ones again. A "wake" would be held for the person emigrating as an opportunity to exchange final goodbyes in anticipation of them never returning home.

windeáil NOUN

(wine-dawl)

winding

The art of ***windeáil*** is an extremely intimate tradition associated with *sean-nós* (traditional Irish) singing. ***Windeáil*** involves the person who is singing taking the hands of another member of the crowd to create a multifaceted connection; a connection between the physical bodies of the two people, a connection to the lyrics, emotions, and shared experiences. The person who is singing leads the ***windeáil***, as the emotions are theirs to express for the duration of the song, and the person listening follows their lead. When the hands of the two parties are intertwined, they move around in a circle, similar to the motion of rowing a boat. However, there is no set rhythm or pattern associated with ***windéail***, as the motions are dictated by the flow of emotions awoken within the singer. The word ***windeáil*** means "winding," and the counterclockwise circular hand movements represent the idea of "winding back the clocks" to honor those before who sang these same songs. Given that *sean-nós* songs cover emotional themes such as grief, famine, love, and loss, ***windeáil*** is a beautiful custom that allows the singer, or custodian of the song, to further engage their listeners and encourage them to sit with the emotions of the song and connect to those who sang them hundreds of years ago.

6 Blessings, Curses, and Proverbs

Irish curses certainly pack a punch, as you will see in this chapter. On the flip side, Irish blessings are a thing of beauty. The word *as Gaeilge* for "proverb" is *seanfhocal*, literally translating to "old word." The Irish are renowned historically and in present day for being an extremely wise nation, and this wisdom is bestowed upon those far and wide through their proverbs. Many of the Irish proverbs possess a figurative meaning, similar to proverbs in other cultures; however, the literal translations often yield a far more interesting explanation.

Aithníonn ciaróg ciaróg eile PROVERB

(ah-NEE-in KEER-oig KEER-oig EHL-eh)

It takes one to know one

The proverb ***Aithníonn ciaróg ciaróg eile*** is most accurately equated to the English proverbs "It takes one to know one," "Like recognizes like," and "Birds of a feather flock together." However, the literal word-for-word translation of this proverb is vastly different than its figurative meanings. ***Aithníonn ciaróg ciaróg eile*** literally translates to "a beetle recognizes another beetle." Where does the beetle come from? Who knows. It's easy enough to know how and when to use this proverb. This proverb can be used in circumstances where you have encountered a kindred spirit—someone that you can connect with instantly and within whom you can identify similar traits and characteristics to yourself. Similarly, in group settings, if two parties in particular hit it off and have the same vibe, it would be true to say in that scenario that ***aithníonn ciaróg ciaróg eile***. This proverb can also be used in a dismissive manner. For example, if someone has fallen into the wrong crowd or has found themselves in less-than-desirable company and is up to no good, well, ***aithníonn ciaróg ciaróg eile***. People are intrinsically drawn to the comfort of familiarity and this remains true regarding the people they align themselves with. If you haven't yet found your flock, just have faith in the idea that your beetle is out there somewhere.

An áit thíos atá ceapaithe duit CURSE

(on AAW-ich heeis ah-THAW CYAP-ee-eh gwitch)

The place below is in store for you

As far as *Gaeilge* is concerned, it's impossible to escape phrases that include a form of religious imagery or connotation—good, bad, or indifferent. When it comes to *an áit thíos*, meaning "the place below," it's not hard to guess that refers to the Christian "hell," or eternal damnation. And so, if an Irish person tells you "***An áit thíos atá ceapaithe duit***," it's plain to see that they view you as morally reprehensible. This phrase's power lies in its simplicity and directness; it leaves no room for misinterpretation and conveys a stark warning of impending doom. It's essentially saying, if you continue with your current actions, there's only one place you'll end up. Or, perhaps it is too late, and your fate has already been decided. In a religious context, it represents a judgment based on perceived moral failings or disobedience to divine law. The person who uses this phrase positions themselves as an authority, pronouncing a sentence of damnation. *An áit thíos* might not always refer to a literal place of eternal torment but rather to a metaphorical state of extreme suffering, misfortune, or retribution. You could use this curse as a warning to express to the other party to change their ways before the path they're on ultimately leads them to *an áit thíos*.

An donas amach, an sonas isteach PROVERB

(on DUH-nis ah-MACKH, on SUH-nis ihs-JACKH)

Out with the bad, in with the good

You can incorporate this proverb into your daily routine, whether it's through meditation, functional breathing, a coping strategy, or just as a positive reminder. ***An donas amach, an sonas isteach*** yields true to its literal translation of "out with the bad, in with the good." When times get tough or you find yourself flustered, take a moment to yourself and call upon the *Gaeilge* gods for some calmness and clarity. Exhale *an donas amach*, and inhale *an sonas isteach*. You're exhaling the bad from your system, and inhaling the good.

In a broader sense, *sonas* can translate to "happiness," "good luck," and "good fortune." *Donas* can be translated to "ill luck," "misfortune," and "misery." This proverb reminds you that struggles will come, but they also will pass and you should make room for the positives in life.

S and D Opposites There are many Irish words starting with the letter *s* that mean something positive. Yet, the same word starting with the letter *d* instead means the opposite negative thing. *Saoirse (seer-shah)* means "freedom," whereas *daoirse (deer-shah)* means "captivity." *Sorcha (sur-kah)* means "bright," whereas *dorcha (dur-kah)* means "darkness." This linguistic trait shows that there are always two sides to the coin, and where there is negativity, there is reflective positivity (or vice versa).

An rud is annamh is iontach PROVERB

(*on rudh iss AWN-oo iss een-tockh*)

What's seldom is wonderful

An rud is annamh is iontach is a cult-classic proverb among the Irish, and the circumstances in which it can be used are endless. The literal translation from *Gaeilge* to *Béarla* reads as "The thing that is rare is wonderful," and the colloquial English translation is "What's seldom is wonderful." This proverb shines a light on the beauty found in special moments in life that don't come often, but when they do, they spread joy to those everywhere. For example, on the occasion that you wrangle the whole friend group together with nobody having conflicting plans or commitments, it would be true to say that ***an rud is annamh is iontach***. When the good weather finally strikes in Ireland and it calls for an impromptu beach day or family barbecue, imagine yourself stretched out with a nice cold drink and let the proverb ***An rud is annamh is iontach*** roll from your tongue. If you manage to find a few peaceful moments from your typically busy schedule and get the opportunity to snuggle up and watch your favorite show or read a book, that moment certainly deserves an iteration of ***an rud is annamh is iontach***. This proverb encourages you not only to appreciate the rare, wonderful moments in life but also to take a moment to appreciate them in their glory.

An té a bhíonn siúlach, bíonn sé scéalach PROVERB

(on tay ah VEE-un SHOE-luckh, BEE-uhn shay SHKAY-luckh)

He who travels has stories to tell

Let this proverb encourage you to get out there, seize the day, and not wait for amazing moments to magically come your way. Then, share your stories. Literally translated, this proverb reads "He who is walking is news-bearing," or "He who travels has stories to tell." This can be interpreted both literally and on a metaphorical level. Literally, if you travel, you'll inevitably have some interesting encounters and you can then share stories about your experiences when you get home. In a metaphorical sense, the "traveling" can refer to the great journey of life. Therefore, if you live life courageously and push yourself out of your comfort zone, you will encounter moments of great excitement and reward.

St. Brendan the Navigator St. Brendan the Navigator was an Irish explorer whose fearlessness earned him the title as the patron saint of the US Navy. He is believed to have embarked on a journey to the land that would become the United States almost one thousand years before Christopher Columbus set sail. His courage to venture into unchartered waters and unknown circumstances earned him notoriety among explorers and sailors across the globe, and his feast day is celebrated on May 16.

Ar dheis Dé go raibh a (h)anam BLESSING

(air yesh djay guh ruh ah [H]AAN-um)

May (she) he rest in peace

The Irish phrase ***Ar dheis Dé go raibh a (h)anam*** is a common expression of sympathy and prayer offered upon the death of someone. This is a beautiful, heartfelt sentiment deeply rooted in Irish Catholic tradition. *Ar dheis Dé* translates to "on the right-hand side of God." In Christian theology, being at God's right hand signifies a place of honor, favor, and eternal peace. It suggests a blessed afterlife for the deceased. The latter section of this phrase, *go raibh a (h)anam*, translates to "may (her) his soul be." Therefore, this phrase in full literally translates to "May (her) his soul be at the right-hand side of God." As per the grammatical rules used to express possession *as Gaeilge*, the letter *h* is added to the beginning of words with a vowel when the item belongs to a woman. Therefore, ***ar dheis Dé go raibh a hanam*** refers to "may she rest in peace" and ***ar dheis Dé go raibh a anam*** refers to "may he rest in peace."

While traditional in a religious context, the phrase is widely used across Ireland, even by those who may not be strictly religious. It serves as a respectful and compassionate way to acknowledge the passing of a loved one and express hopes for a peaceful afterlife. The sentiment of wishing someone peace and comfort after death transcends specific religious beliefs, making it a universally understood expression of sympathy.

Ar scáth a chéile a mhaireann na daoine PROVERB

(air skaw ah KHAYL-a ah WAARR-en nah DEE-nah)

In one another's shadows, we prosper

There are a few ways in which the proverb ***Ar scáth a chéile a mhaireann na daoine*** can be translated and interpreted; it's a phrase that is beautiful *as Gaeilge*, but the translations just don't hit the same. Many Irish proverbs have a reflective English equivalent that carries the same essence, but this is not one of them. The word *scáth* itself means "shade" or "shadow," so *ar scáth a chéile* translates to "in one another's shadow / shade." The latter part, *a mhaireann na daoine* means "people survive" or "people live." So, when put all together, the phrase translates to "in one another's shadow, we survive." ***Ar scáth a chéile a mhaireann na daoine*** basically implies that people need each other to survive, and communities depend on each other; individuals are all living in the shadow of each other, meaning that no one walks alone. This proverb captures the essence of community, people coming together, and the beauty that lies within it.

The Shadow People **The belief in "shadow people" is deep-rooted in Irish mythology and folklore. Shadows are believed to be physical presentation of *AntAlltar* ("The Otherworld") and serve as a link between the mortals and the dead. Although the belief in shadow people is not exclusive to Ireland, these dark entities lurk in the background as omens of darkness and death, similar to other Irish mythological beings like the banshee.**

Cuireann tú fonn múisce orm CURSE

(KWUIHR-in too fown MOOSH-ce UR-um)

You make me want to vomit; you sicken me

At some point, you may have had the misfortune of encountering someone who quite literally makes you feel sick. ***Cuireann tú fonn múise orm*** is the perfect curse here. *As Gaeilge*, the word *fonn* refers to a "desire," "wish," "inclination," or "urge." *Múisc (mooshk)* is the word used to refer to "vomit," "nausea," or "loathing." Appropriately, the word *múisc* itself sounds like a sound you'd make while emptying your stomach over a toilet. Therefore, when you put the whole phrase ***Cuireann tú fonn múisce orm*** together, it means "You put a desire to vomit upon me." If you're brave enough, feel free to say this right to someone's face, but if you wish to be a bit more discreet and say this behind someone's back, you can swap out the *tú* for *sé* (he), *sí* (she), or *siad* (they).

Flat 7 Up **Possibly the most infamous "cure" in Irish culture is flat 7 Up. If you're feeling nauseous, have a glass of flat 7 Up. Have a headache? Glass of flat 7 Up coming up. Any other ailment that can't be cured? Sure, a glass of flat 7 Up won't do you any harm. Flat 7 Up simply refers to decarbonated 7 Up that has been either boiled or left to sit for a while. There is no scientific evidence that proves the healing powers of flat 7 Up, but who needs science when you have cultural belief.**

Cuir síoda ar ghabhar, is gabhar fós é PROVERB

(kwur SHEE-i-dah air GHOW-er, iss gow-er i gon-ee ay)

Put silk on a goat, it's still a goat

You can't help but chuckle at this proverb. ***Cuir síoda ar ghabhar, is gabhar fós é*** translates to "Put silk on a goat, it's still a goat," but what can you infer from these words of comical wisdom? In essence, this proverb says that you can't paint someone, something, or a situation out to be something that it's not. No matter how hard you try, you can't change or alter someone's true self. If someone is nasty or cruel at their core, even though they might put on a smile and a portray a welcoming nature, they're still a nasty person. So, they're still a goat but just a goat dressed in silk.

This proverb can be used in a not-so-nice way to comment on someone's physical appearance, that someone is wearing makeup or particular clothing in an effort to embellish their appearance. However, in a more positive spin, this proverb can serve as a message of empowerment to accept who you truly are. Don't bother wasting your time wrapping yourself in silk and trying to hide your true self, embrace yourself as the silkless goat you are. It doesn't sound as empowering when you put it that way . . . but nonetheless, trust that the sentiment is there.

Dá fhada an lá, tagann an oíche PROVERB

(daw awhd-ah on law, TAWG-in on EE-cha)

However long the day is, night will come

This proverb suggests that no matter what, there is always light at the end of the tunnel. ***Dá fhada an lá, tagann an oíche*** translates to "However long the day is, night will come." It's a beautiful short-term reminder that even the toughest and busiest of days will come to an end, the sun will set, and you'll get to rest your head on your pillow and drift off to sleep. Looking at this proverb in a broader context, it urges you to remember that hard times will come, but there is an end in sight, and as the sun sets, so do you. You will get the opportunity to move forward symbolically into a new day and into a new chapter of your life. Today, ***Dá fhada an lá, tagann an oíche*** can be seen adorned on clothing items such as hats, tote bags, jewelry, and jumpers, as the masses can relate to and find peace in the sentiment of this proverb. An alternate version for ***Dá fhada an lá, tagann an oíche*** is *Dá fhada an lá, tagann an tráthnóna*, which translates to "However long the day is, evening will come." Although the two versions are basically the same, you can choose to use and call upon whichever you feel brings you the most comfort in times of uncertainty.

deiseal BLESSING

(DEH-shul)

clockwise; blessed; "bless you" after sneezing

In the Irish language, the word ***deiseal*** has a dual meaning, referring both to "clockwise" and "right-handed." This connection is reflected in its use as a traditional response to a sneeze, as an Irish "bless you!" The Irish believe that movements in a clockwise direction are associated with good luck and positive outcomes. This offers a glimpse into the cultural significance of the Irish language and its connection to traditional beliefs and practices. The preference for clockwise movement, or ***deiseal***, in Irish culture is deeply rooted in ancient traditions. The practice is linked to several key concepts; the sun's apparent journey across the sky is from east to west, and thus, ***deiseal*** motion mimics the sun's life-giving energy and cyclical nature. With this comes positive energy, growth, and prosperity. Many cultures believe that moving clockwise creates a protective barrier against negative influences. In Irish tradition, they believed this movement was a way to ward off malevolent spirits or bad luck. The act of walking ***deiseal*** around a sacred site, such as a holy well or standing stone, was believed to enhance the site's protective power. This practice is evident in many traditional Irish customs. Some agricultural practices, like sowing seeds or harvesting crops, were traditionally performed following a ***deiseal*** pattern.

Doras feasa fiafraí PROVERB

(DHUHR-iss fahs-a fee-ah-free)

Questioning is the door to wisdom

The evocative Irish proverb ***Doras feasa fiafraí*** encapsulates that the path to knowledge begins with the act of questioning. When broken down, the three individual words of this phrase mean the following: *doras* = door, *feasa* = wisdom, and *fiafraí* = questioning. It's not about passively receiving information, but actively seeking it out. The *doras* represents the gateway to understanding, and *fiafraí* is the key that unlocks it.

While pinpointing the phrase's precise origin is difficult, its essence aligns with the long-standing Irish tradition of storytelling, debate, and intellectual curiosity. The emphasis on questioning reflects a culture in Ireland, both historically and in modern day, that values critical thinking and the pursuit of truth. The ancient Celtic bards are a prime example; their rhymes and riddles stimulated minds and prompted never-ending inquiry and intrigue. The proverb ***Doras feasa fiafraí*** encourages a proactive approach to learning. It's a call to challenge assumptions, seek clarification, and explore the unknown. After all, the journey of learning is a continuous process of questioning, refining, and expanding your understanding. So, this proverb is a testament to the power of curiosity and the importance of seeking one's inner Socrates, never ceasing to ask "Why?"

Filleann an feall ar an bhfeallaire PROVERB

(FIHL-enn on fahl air on VIAHL-er-ah)

The treachery returns to the betrayer

Filleann an feall ar an bhfeallaire translates figuratively to "evil returns to the evil-doer," or "treachery returns to the betrayer." This proverb conceptualizes karma, suggesting that wrongdoing will ultimately result in negative consequences for the perpetrator. Now, this isn't necessarily a supernatural or divine judgment, but rather a recognition that deceitful or harmful actions often create a ripple effect, leading to negative outcomes for the person who initiated them. This could manifest in various ways: damaged relationships, loss of trust, or even legal consequences. In modern interpretations, the proverb's message of "what goes around comes around" remains relevant. It's a cautionary reminder about the importance of ethical behavior and the potential consequences of acting with malice or deceit.

While the concept of karma may be viewed through different lenses, the underlying principle of accountability remains central. The concept of ***filleann an feall ar an bhfeallaire*** encourages reflection on your actions and their potential impact, urging you to consider the long-term consequences before engaging in harmful acts. While immediate gains from wrongdoing might seem appealing, the ultimate price to be paid in the future may be far greater. The proverb's enduring presence in Irish culture underscores its continuing wisdom and relevance in navigating life's complexities.

Giorraíonn beirt bóthar PROVERB

(gyuhr-ee-uhn bert-ch bow-her)

Two shorten a road

This old Irish saying, ***Giorraíonn beirt bóthar***, translates to "Two shorten a road." *Giorraíonn* is the verb "to shorten," *beirt* is the word used to refer to "two people" specifically (counting people in Irish requires a different numerical system), and *bóthar* is the word for "road." As many Irish proverbs can, ***Giorraíonn beirt bóthar*** can be seen literally and metaphorically. If you're out on a stroll or on a drive by yourself, it may feel as though you're not covering ground very quickly and the journey might drag on. However, if you have company, the constant chit-chat can make the journey go by quickly. Metaphorically, this proverb says that "a problem shared is a problem halved." The *bóthar* can refer to any of life's journeys, which can be shortened or eased by the help of others. In other words, don't be afraid to ask people to accompany you on either a leisurely stroll or on the journey of life itself.

Follow the Cows! The word *bóthar* for "road" *as Gaeilge* when broken down literally translates to "cow path." Many of the winding roads still used by motorists in rural areas of Ireland were originally paved by following the natural paths cows would take when traveling from one place to another. This might not have been the most practical or ergonomic approach, but there's no justification to question the cows' wisdom.

Go dtite an bháisteach go mín ar do pháirceanna BLESSING

(guh dit-eh on vawsh-tukh guh meen air duh FAWRK-inn-ah)

May the rains fall softly upon your fields

Go dtite an bháisteach go mín ar do pháirceanna, translating to "May the rain fall softly on your fields," is a beautiful Irish blessing that conveys heartfelt wishes for abundance and prosperity. In the context of Irish culture, this phrase is rich with agricultural significance, reflecting the deep connection between the land of Ireland and its people. The phrase highlights the Irish reverence for nature in a country known for its lush green landscapes. This blessing acknowledges the importance of favorable weather for farming and sustenance, and it embodies the spirit of community and support by wishing that your crops thrive and flourish. Although Ireland is now commonly perceived as an extremely wet country, this wasn't always the case. Historically, the country would experience periods of low rainfall, and drought would ensue, detrimental to crop growth. Therefore, wishing rainfall upon someone's fields was viewed as the height of blessings.

How Rainy Is Ireland, Actually? Believe it or not, Ireland is not among the countries in the world with the highest levels of rainfall per year. Typically, Ireland ranks somewhere in the eighties on the list of rainfall by country. Although the rainfall in Ireland isn't as heavy as that of tropical countries, it feels constant and relentless. In general, it rains 151 to 225 days each year, making it feel like there's a light, constant shower.

Go hifreann leat CURSE

(guh hih-frinn lyat)

To hell with you

Ifreann refers to both the fiery realm of hell, but also the "Otherworld" at large. The word *ifreann* stems from the Old Irish word *ifernn*, which is derived from the Latin *infernus*. ***Go hifreann leat!*** (meaning "to hell with you") is a heated phrase often used in Ireland to convey intense feelings of anger, frustration, or dismissal toward someone. It's akin to saying "Go to hell!" and reflects a desire to cut ties or express disdain for the person being addressed. This phrase is typically used when someone feels wronged or deeply upset. It serves as a way to forcibly assert boundaries, indicating that the speaker no longer wishes to engage with the person in question. In exclaiming "***Go hifreann leat!***" to someone, you are asserting a wish for not only a physical distance between yourself and the other party, but a spiritual distance also. In Irish culture, where humor and directness often intertwine, such expressions can be used both seriously and playfully. The phrase might be employed in a heated argument or as a lighthearted jab among friends, depending on the tone and context. Using this phrase can provide a sense of relief for the speaker, allowing them to express their feelings openly. It's a way to reclaim power in a situation where someone feels disrespected or hurt.

Go lagfaidh Dia thú CURSE

(guh LAWG-eh JEE-eh hoo)

May God strike you

Across various Christian and Catholic traditions and cultures, it is often the case that someone may say, "May God strike you." In the Irish language, the equivalent curse is ***Go lagfaidh Dia thú***. This exclamation carries the intention of God putting manners on said person, asking God to give them a hard and stern reason to correct their ways. In a more figurative and modern sense, it means: "May some divine power slap you in the face and make you realize your wrongdoings." Expressing "***Go lagfaidh Dia thú***" to someone would happen when you are immensely angry and wish for something, or someone, to come down from the clouds above and knock some sense into that person for once and for all. Of course, using this curse won't actually result in any physical harm being inflicted on the person, but the sentiment rings true.

Fear the Wooden Spoon Older generations of Irish fear the wooden spoon, and this fear has been passed down to younger generations through the stories told by their parents and grandparents. A home's wooden spoon would be used to strike or discipline a child. Nowadays, the phrase "don't make me get the wooden spoon" is used as a playful warning, getting the children to quit a behavior.

Go maire tú an céad BLESSING

(guh maa-reh thoo on khaydh)

May you live to be a hundred years old

The Irish phrase ***Go maire tú an céad*** translates literally to "May you live to a hundred." It's a simple, powerful expression of goodwill and longevity, frequently used to convey well wishes, particularly on birthdays. While pinpointing its exact origin is difficult, its roots lie deep within Irish culture's emphasis on community and the importance of long life. The desire for a long life isn't merely about reaching a specific age, as it represents a hope for experiencing life's fullness, witnessing familial growth, and contributing to the community. In modern Ireland, the phrase remains a cherished expression. It's used informally among friends and family, and it maintains its traditional warmth and sincerity. This phrase isn't a polite formality; it conveys genuine affection and the hope for continued health and happiness. It's a simple wish for a long and prosperous life, a sentiment that resonates across generations and cultural contexts.

Birthday Wishes from the President In Ireland, there's a lovely tradition known as the Centenarian Bounty, where individuals who reach their hundredth birthday receive a special congratulatory letter signed by *Uachtarán na hÉireann*, the President of Ireland, along with a monetary gift of €2,540. Recipients also receive a commemorative coin as part of the celebration. This tradition began in 2000 and aims to honor the remarkable milestone of reaching a century.

Go ndéana an diabhal dréimire de chnámh do dhroma CURSE

(guh nyayn-eh on dj-owl draym-reh de knawv dhuh ghruma)

May God make a ladder from your spine

Of all the Irish curses in this chapter, ***Go ndéana an diabhal dréimire de chnámh do dhroma*** is certainly the most graphic and gruesome. "May the devil make a ladder from the bones of your back" is quite the colorful and vivid expression from Irish folklore. This phrase, like many Irish curses, carries historical and cultural significance. The phrase conjures a graphic image, suggesting that the recipient will face significant hardship or misfortune. A ladder made from human bones implies a painful and arduous journey, often associated with betrayal or deep frustration. This particular curse reflects the intensity of feelings that can arise in interpersonal conflicts. It's not just a casual insult; it's an extremely serious expression of ill will. You might hear this phrase in moments of extreme frustration or when someone feels deeply wronged. This phrase may be used when strong emotions are at play among close acquaintances, or when wrongdoing has been carried out by a relative, which is seen as one of the worst kinds of betrayal in Ireland. Nowadays, such phrases are less commonly used in actuality and are often viewed with a sense of humor or nostalgia. They reflect the rich tapestry of Irish linguistic tradition, where even curses can be poetic and deeply expressive.

Go n-imí an drochaimsir leat CURSE

(guh nim-ee on drukh-aym-shur lyat)

May bad weather follow you

Irish people don't take the topic of weather lightly. As a people, the Irish contain an innate disdain toward bad weather in particular, as it often ruins plans. ***Go n-imí an drochaimsir leat*** is a colorful and somewhat humorous saying in Ireland, often used as a playful retort or a lighthearted jab. This "curse" is typically directed at someone who frequently complains about the weather. It's a cheeky way to suggest that if they are so focused on the negative aspects of the weather, they might as well have the bad weather stick around them like a bad smell. The Irish are known for their wit and humor, and this expression reflects that. This phrase is not meant to be taken literally (because the Irish can't *actually* control the weather); rather, it's a way to poke fun at someone's tendency to complain.

Interestingly, there is *another* expression common in Ireland to do with the weather following someone: *Tá an aimsir tugtha leat (taw on aym-shur tugha lyat)*, translating to "You've brought the weather with you." This phrase is typically directed at someone who has arrived home from abroad, particularly somewhere with a steadier temperate climate than Ireland, and then Ireland experiences better than normal weather. This implies that the traveler, themself, has brought such weather home. Maybe the Irish can control the weather after all?

Go séideadh an diabhal san aer thú CURSE

(guh shayd-eh on dj-owl san air hoo)

May the devil blow you into the air

This expression is a great example of the vibrant language rooted in Irish folklore. It draws on traditional imagery, with *an diabhal* representing mischief or trouble, and being blown into the air, painting a picture of someone being tossed into chaos or uncertainty. Used mostly in moments of frustration, this phrase is more like having a dig at someone than an actual curse. So, you might say this when someone's done something daft or mildly irritating; it's a humorous way of showing annoyance without any real malice behind it. You'll often hear it in casual banter, or as the Irish call it, having the *craic*, particularly among friends or family teasing each other. It adds a bit of theatrical fun to everyday conversation. Though not as common in modern speech, the phrase carries a certain charm.

An Fear Dubh One way of referring to "the devil" *as Gaeilge* is *an diabhal*, but another option is the term *An Fear Dubh*. This literally translates to "the black man," but colors are used differently in Irish than in English. The word *dubh* is associated with the color "black," but the word refers to darkness at large—not just a shade. Therefore, *An Fear Dubh* means "The Dark Man," which sounds like an accurate depiction of the devil himself.

I dtosach na haicíde is fusa í a leigheas PROVERB

(ih dusukh nah hah-keyd-eh iss fuhsa ee a lie-ihs)

It is at the beginning of a disease it is easiest to cure

I dtosach na haicíde is fusa í a leigheas is an Irish proverb that teaches you a valuable lesson. Directly translating to "It is at the beginning of a disease it is easiest to cure," this phrase holds the same essence as "Prevention is better than a cure." This proverb is often heard in reference to politics, and people in power are urged to tackle issues before they grow out of control. Tackle the issue at its root, before it morphs into something worse that could have been minimized with appropriate strategy and planning. This proverb can be implemented into anyone's life; instead of brushing issues under the rug and intending to deal with them later, confront them now. Though this proverb isn't referring to a literal disease, think of challenges and issues in your life as a disease. Instead of letting them fester in your body, grow, mutate, and spread, find the root of the issue and treat it as soon as possible. Irish proverbs have rightfully gained notoriety for their wisdom, and their associated principles and recommendations should be adhered to and put into practice. So, no matter what, remember that ***i dtosach na haicíde is fusa í a leigheas***.

Imeacht gan do thuairisc ort CURSE

(ihm-ukt gawn duh hoor-ishk urt)

May you disappear without a trace

This Irish curse, ***Imeacht gan do thuairisc ort***, translates literally to "Leave without report on you" and figuratively to "May you disappear without a trace," and it carries quite a devastating weight behind it. While seemingly benign, it functions as a potent curse, invoking the fear of oblivion and the severing of ties to the past. The curse likely stems from a cultural context valuing lineage and communal memory. Disappearing without a trace would have been a significant social transgression, denying your place within the community and family history. *Gan do thuairisc ort* represents physical absence and the erasure of your identity and contributions, a form of ultimate social death. Capturing in essence what Ernest Hemingway would later inscribe, "Every man has two deaths: when he is buried in the ground and the last time someone says his name." While ***Imeacht gan do thuairisc ort*** may not invoke immediate physical harm upon someone, it functions as a social curse, threatening the loss of identity, memory, and connection. It's a potent reminder of the importance of community, legacy, and the lasting impact individuals have on those around them. The curse's power lies in its subtle threat of complete erasure from the collective consciousness.

Im ná raibh ar do bhainne CURSE

(ihm naaw ruh air duh vawn-yeh)

May your milk not make butter

Im ná raibh ar do bhainne is one of the pettier curses *as Gaeilge*. Although it doesn't intend to inflict eternal damnation or a one-way ticket to hell, it's still evil. This curse literally translates to "May your milk not make butter," which yields the equally literal sentiment of wishing an eternity of churning upon the person you wish to curse. Petty, right? This curse is not intended to cause actual harm but rather to express a wish for misfortune, lack of success, and inconvenience. Historically, butter-making was a crucial part of rural Irish life. It was a source of income and sustenance, so the inability to yield butter from churning represented significant hardship; the curse ***Im ná raibh ar do bhainne*** plays on this.

To Roll the *N* or Not The pronunciation of the letter *n as Gaeilge* will vary between dialects. The most notable difference is in the Munster dialect where the *n* sound is not rolled. In Ulster and Connacht dialects, the *n* is similar to the *ñ* in Spanish, which would lead to a word such as *bainne* being sounded as *(bawn-yah)*. However, in the Munster dialect, *bainne* would be sounded as *(bawn-ah)*. Homing in on this difference in pronunciation is just one way to differentiate between dialects.

I ndiaidh a chéile a thógtar na caisleáin PROVERB

(ih NYEE-eh ah khayl-eh ah HOEG-thur na kuish-lawn)

Bit by bit the castle is built

The proverb ***I ndiaidh a chéile a thógtar na caisleáin*** is most comparable to the English phrase "Rome wasn't built in a day." *I ndiaidh a chéile* translates to "bit by bit" and *a thógtar na caisleáin* translates to "the castles are built." This phrase urges you to reflect on the fact that nothing happens overnight and good things take time to come to fruition. If you have a seemingly unachievable feat ahead, break it down into smaller tasks and tackle it bit by bit. By placing these individual bricks gradually, you will one day build your castle and be able to stand back to admire what you have built for yourself. In focusing on the essence of this proverb, you are focusing on the skills of patience and foresight. Although something may seem impossible now, have faith that in a few days, weeks, months, or years down the line, everything will come together as it should. This is another phrase that you could incorporate into reflective practices in your everyday life. Take a deep breath in, look at yourself in the mirror, and utter the words ***I ndiaidh a chéile a thógtar na caisleáin*** to yourself.

Is binn béal ina thost PROVERB

(iss bin bayl ihn-a husth)

Silence is golden

This Irish proverb has two comparable equivalents in English that are widely recognized, but from a completely unbiased perspective, ***Is binn béal ina thost*** is far nicer. This literally translates to "Sweet is a mouth that is silent," or more figuratively, "Silence is golden." *Binn* is the adjective used in this proverb to refer to "sweet," but more specifically refers to a sound that is sweet. *Milis (mih-lish)* is the word *as Gaeilge* to refer to a sweet taste, but it is clear that this proverb refers to the sound of silence that is sweet, as opposed to the taste of the silence itself. The equivalent in English would be "A closed mouth never catches a fly" or "If you don't have anything nice to say, don't say anything at all." In essence, this proverb serves to remind you that sometimes it is better to bite your tongue, however hard it may be, instead of speaking from a place of anger, landing yourself in further trouble down the line. If you happen to find yourself hotheaded with an insult or nasty remark at the tip of your tongue, stop and ask yourself which will be sweeter: the satisfaction of voicing the nasty remark, or the sweetness of being the bigger person and keeping it to yourself?

Is fearr an tsláinte ná na táinte PROVERB

(iss fyar on ts-lawin-cha naw nah tawin-te)

Our health is better than your wealth

Irish people cherish their health greatly and this sentiment can be seen reflected in blessings, proverbs, and toasts *as Gaeilge*. For example, as seen in Chapter 3, *sláinte*, which means "cheers" when raising a glass, translates to "health." The word *sláinte* pops up again in this proverb. ***Is fearr an tsláinte ná na táinte*** rolls off the tongue due to its beautiful rhyme between *sláinte* and *táinte* meaning "wealth." The word *táinte* in its root form *táin* originally referred to a vast herd of cattle, which would have traditionally been used to measure wealth in Ireland among farmers and broader communities. Therefore, the concept of placing value on health as opposed to monetary wealth is not a new idea; it's a value that has stuck with Irish people for hundreds of years. In an age where your value can be measured by your car, having the latest model of iPhone, and adorning yourself with designer items, let this proverb serve as a reminder to you that ***Is fearr an tsláinte ná na táinte***, and at the end of the day, you can't put a price on good health.

Is glas iad na cnoic i bhfad uainn PROVERB

(iss glaws ee-ud nah krick ih wawd oo-ihn)

Faraway hills are green

The infamous Irish proverb ***Is glas iad na cnoic i bhfad uainn*** speaks to the human tendency to idealize the distant and unknown. So, things often appear more attractive or desirable when viewed from a distance, while their realities may be less appealing upon closer examination. The imagery of green hills evokes a sense of beauty, tranquility, and opportunity. The proverb likely emerged from a common human experience and observation of behaviors. The distant hills, shrouded in mist or haze, appear idyllic, their imperfections obscured by distance. This visual effect mirrors the common tendency to romanticize the unknown, to focus on the positive aspects while overlooking potential challenges.

The proverb's application is broad. It can refer to relationships, career choices, or even geographical relocation. The grass always seems greener and lusher on the other side. The proverb also serves as a cautionary reminder. It encourages a more balanced and realistic perspective, urging you to examine your desires and aspirations critically, to move beyond superficial attractions and consider the full picture before making decisions. It promotes introspection and a mindful approach to life's choices, suggesting that happiness is not always found in distant lands or unattainable dreams, but rather in appreciating the present and recognizing the beauty in what is near.

Is maith an scéalaí an aimsir PROVERB

(iss mawh on shkay-lee on AHM-sher)

The weather is a good storyteller

Is maith an scéalaí an aimsir translates to "Weather is a good storyteller"; the keywords being *scéalaí*, "storyteller," and *aimsir*, "weather." This proverb highlights the Irish people's observation of the natural world, particularly the ever-changing weather patterns. The proverb suggests that the weather, with its shifts and cycles, reveals much about the environment and the human experience. ***Is maith an scéalaí an aimsir*** reflects the agricultural and maritime heritage of Ireland, where understanding the weather was crucial for survival and livelihood. The proverb's meaning is multilayered, suggesting that the weather tells a story of seasons changing, storms brewing, and the land's response to sun and rain. It also implies that the weather influences the lives of people, shaping their activities, moods, and even their conversations. For example, Irish fishermen were known to closely observe seagull behavior to predict the weather. Seagulls flying high in the sky was an indicator of a storm to come. (In the now-understood scientific context, the birds' activity before a storm is a response to heightened atmospheric pressure and wind patterns.) The fishermen's study of seagull activity allowed them to anticipate dangerous weather conditions and decide whether or not it would be safe to set sail. This generational knowledge demonstrates a deep understanding of the natural world.

Lao ná raibh ag do bhó CURSE

(lee naaw ruh egg duh voah)

May your cow not calf

Wishing calfless cows upon someone is a new level of low. *Lao* is the word *as Gaeilge* for "calf," and *do bhó* translates to "your cow." *Ná raibh* in this case can be translated to "may not." Therefore, expressing ***lao ná raibh ag do bhó*** upon someone is condemning their cows to not produce calves. To this day, Ireland is one of the foremost milk producers in the world due to the country's favorable climate for dairy farming. The *bó* was first brought to Ireland by the Neolithic people, and it quickly became an integral aspect of survival and livelihood. They were the most precious animal on Irish farms and were linked heavily to many mythological beliefs. A *cros Bhríde* (St. Brigid's cross) was hung in the cow house to protect the livestock and the food products they would yield. It's said that all cattle in Ireland descend from the first three cows brought to the island by a beautiful maiden of the sea. These three cows were named after their individual colors: *Bó Finn*, "the white cow"; *Bó Rua*, "the red cow"; and *Bó Dubh*, "the black cow." Having a white cow on a farm is believed to be bad luck, as the fairy folk would steal this color cow over any another color. Mythological aspects aside, the cows and their milk, butter, and meat were vital to the survival of the Irish people historically, and wishing calfless cows upon a farmer was an extremely cruel curse.

Marú na Sasanach ort CURSE

(maawr-oo nah saws-an-awkh urt)

Death at the hands of an English

The curse reflects a dark period in Irish history marked by conflict and oppression and should not be used lightly or playfully. ***Marú na Sasanach ort*** expresses a wish for misfortune, and, in its most extreme form, death inflicted by an Englishman. This sentiment stems from the historical struggles and grievances between the Irish and the English when the country was under British rule, including events like the Penal Laws, the Great Famine, and various periods of political and military conflict. The phrase encapsulates the pain, resentment, and anger felt by many Irish people toward the English during these difficult times. Half a million Irish people were evicted from their homes by British landowners and were forced to succumb to the elements during the famine of 1845 onward. Plus, much of the little food remaining on the island was exported to Britian. The total death toll of the Great Hunger (also known as the Great Famine) sits at approximately one million people, and given that this tragic period occurred less than two hundred years ago, it remains a topic of ongoing reflection and discussion in modern Ireland. To die at the hands of an Englishman is part of Ireland's turbulent past, and therefore this curse should be reserved for those who betray you in the most significant sense.

Mol an óige agus tiocfaidh sí PROVERB

(mull on oh-ihg-eh aw-guhs chuck-ee she)

Praise the youth and they will prosper

Mol an óige agus tiocfaidh sí is a proverb that serves to remind people of the importance of encouraging the youth and fostering young minds and talent. *Mol* is the verb "to praise" or "to commend," *an óige* is "the youth," and *agus tiocfaidh sí* means "and she will prosper." "She" is used because *óige* (the youth) is a feminine noun. Praising the youth and providing safe spaces for them to explore both their talents and weaknesses allows young minds to grow and learn. This proverb encourages you not only to celebrate children's achievements but also to foster their interests. After all, the youth are the next generation of the world, and the future lies in their hands. ***Mol an óige agus tiocfaidh sí*** is often used as a motto or mantra at schools and childcare facilities across Ireland.

The Most Educated Country in the World In 2025, Ireland was ranked as the most educated country in the world: 52.4 percent of the population aged 25 to 64, equating to 1.8 million people, were recorded as having a bachelor's degree or higher. Given that there are only twenty-five universities and third-level institutions and a handful of further education centers in the country, this ranking as the most educated country in the world is outstanding.

Mo sheacht mbeannacht ort BLESSING

(muh hyackth mahn-ukth urt)

My seven blessings upon you

The Irish appreciation of numerology stems largely from Celtic traditions and beliefs. The number seven features heavily in these beliefs; it's believed to represent perfect order and bring good luck and fortune. Therefore, the blessing ***Mo sheacht mbeannacht ort***, simply translating to "My seven blessings upon you," reflects the deep-rooted Irish emphasis on communal well-being and spiritual connection. It's a heartfelt expression of goodwill, often used as a farewell or to bestow good fortune upon someone. The seven blessings are not rigidly defined and may include good health, prosperity, love, peace, wisdom, courage, and faith (essentially encompassing the most cherished aspects of life). The number seven is cyclical and represents a complete period or cycle, or, in other words, the aspects of life and humanity that are necessary to keep the world spinning.

The Seven Wonders of Fore You've heard of the Seven Wonders of the World, but what are the Seven Wonders of Fore? Fore Abbey is located in County Westmeath, in the midlands of Ireland, and this seventh-century monastic site has seven wonders of its own. The monastery built on the bog, the mill without a race, the water that flows uphill, the tree that won't burn, the water that won't boil, the anchorite in a stone, and the stone raised by St. Féichín's prayers.

Níl aon tinteán mar do thinteán féin PROVERB

(kneel ayn tin-tawn maar duh hin-tawn fayn)

There's no place like home; there's no hearth like your own hearth

This proverb is the epitome of the Irish fondness for home and the country's innate patriotism. Many Irish proverbs *as Gaeilge* are quite niche to those who speak the language proficiently and are largely familiar with it, but ***Níl aon tinteán mar do thinteán féin*** is seen on posters hung proudly in classrooms across the country. This Irish proverb, translating literally to "There's no hearth like your own hearth," speaks volumes about the importance of home and belonging. This phrase carries deep cultural and emotional weight, often implying a sense of loss or longing when you're far from home; it's similar to the phrase "There's no place like home." The hearth represents warmth, safety, and familial bonds. ***Níl aon tinteán mar do thinteán féin*** reflects a deep yearning for the familiar comforts and emotional security of home.

In modern times, the proverb resonates deeply with those who have emigrated, highlighting the emotional toll of being separated from loved ones and familiar surroundings. It speaks to the enduring power of home, no matter where you travel. The sentiment transcends physical location; it speaks to the emotional anchor that your home provides. It is a reminder of the importance of family, community, and the comforting embrace of well-loved surroundings.

Níl uasal ná íseal ach thuas seal agus thíos seal PROVERB

(kneel oos-ul naw eesh-ul ackh hoo-us shall awgis hee-us shall)

There's no up nor down, just ups and downs

Níl uasal ná íseal ach thuas seal agus thíos seal is a proverb that most need to hear in difficult times. The sentiment of this phrase is truly beautiful. Translating to "There's no up or down, just ups and downs," it's clear to see why this proverb has a special place in the hearts of Irish speakers. It reminds you that when times are tough, nothing lasts forever, and good times will come. In using the proverb ***Níl uasal ná íseal ach thuas seal agus thíos seal***, you are making peace with the roller coaster of emotions that is life. No one knows what's around the corner, but you must remind yourself that it is all part of the wonderfully complicated journey that is life. The latter section of this proverb, *thuas seal agus thíos seal*, can be taken on its own, used in reference to the ups and downs of life. If someone expresses empathy to you in a time of struggle, you can respond with *thuas seal thíos seal* to show them that you are okay and aware of the fact that this is just a tricky time in your life, not a tricky life as a whole.

Níl saoi gan locht PROVERB

(kneel see gawn luckth)

There's no wise man without fault

A *saoi* in the Irish language refers to a wise man, but even he has faults. The proverb ***Níl saoi gan locht*** translates directly to "There is no wise man without fault." This timeless expression highlights the inherent imperfection of even the wisest individuals. It doesn't imply that wise men are flawed in character, but rather acknowledges that wisdom doesn't equate to infallibility. Even the most knowledgeable individuals make mistakes, hold biases, or experience shortcomings in judgment.

The origins are difficult to pinpoint precisely, as many such proverbs evolve organically within a culture's oral tradition. However, its enduring presence in Irish culture suggests a deep-rooted understanding of human nature. The proverb serves as a reminder of humility and self-awareness. It encourages a balanced perspective, not allowing you to place others on a pedestal. This phrase acts as a gentle antidote to the dangers of blind faith or unquestioning obedience. The phrase isn't typically used as a curse per se, but rather as a cautionary observation; it's invoked in situations where someone is being overly critical or judgmental of another's imperfections as a reminder that everyone is fallible. In the modern context, it carries an important message of empathy and understanding. In a world that often glorifies success and perfection, ***Níl saoi gan locht*** encourages you to appreciate humanity in yourself and others, fostering tolerance and acceptance of flaws.

Nimh do bhéil id bhráid CURSE

(niv duh vayl id vraw-id)

May you suffer the same poison you speak

Nimh do bhéil id bhráid is a potent Irish curse rooted in the principle of karmic retribution. It's not a wish for physical harm, but rather a criticism of the speaker's hateful words. The *nimh*, or "poison," in this curse refers to the venomous nature of a person's words, implying they contain deceit, treachery, or slander. The true power of this curse lies in its directness, and it serves as a warning—a prediction of self-inflicted consequences. Unfortunately, in all walks of life, there are times where you'll encounter cruel or negative people. In these cases, you can call upon this curse as both a reminder and a warning that speaking negativity into the world will bring consequences. The curse would have traditionally been used in situations where someone was spreading false rumors or engaging in harmful gossip. In modern day, the curse ***Nimh do bhéil id bhráid*** remains just as relevant, if not more so. Within the digital age and as you immerse yourself in social media, the circumstances in which misinformation can be easily spread are rampant. Think of this curse as a cautionary tale: that you yourself may become as toxic as the words you speak. With the accessibility of spreading information comes great responsibility.

Níor bhris focal maith fiacail riamh PROVERB

(kneer vrish fuk-ill mawh fee-uh-kul REE-uv)

A good word never broke a tooth

The Irish proverb ***Níor bhris focal maith fiacail riamh*** serves as a cautionary tale. This piece of traditional wisdom emphasizes the importance of choosing your words carefully. The proverb's imagery is simple yet effective; the *focal maith*, meaning "good word," references positive actions and kindness at large. This image contrasts with actions that might cause physical harm or retribution, like breaking a tooth. This comparison highlights the benefits of using kind words and the absence of any negative repercussions for doing so. You might perceive this proverb as meaning that speaking negatively about someone or something could lead to conflict, and in the worst-case scenario, physical conflict, resulting in injury. This proverb may be viewed in a "what goes around comes around" sense, meaning that if negative words come from your mouth, you are drawing future misfortune your way. Historically, in Irish society, strong verbal communication skills were highly valued. Diplomacy, cooperation, and the avoidance of conflict through the use of constructive language were encouraged. This is particularly important in a culture that places value on community and interpersonal harmony. On an island that has its fill of characters whose flair and charm are on par with their tempers and agitations, this proverb is a reminder that a cool and wise tongue prevents a fiery and blunt fist.

Nuair a bhíonn an t-ól istigh, bíonn an chiall amuigh PROVERB

(noor ah VEE-un on toll ish-chih, BEE-un on KEE-ull ah-MUH)

When the drink is in, the sense is out

If you're planning a trip to Ireland and are looking for a phrase to justify your potential future drunken antics, ***Nuair a bhíonn an t-ól istigh, bíonn an chiall amuigh*** is the one for you. This proverb means "When the drink is in, the sense is out" and can serve as a playful dig to yourself or a friend; it could also be used to cast judgment on those who lose their own sense of reasonable judgment after a few (too many) drinks. If you've said or done something questionable in your altered mental state, just remind yourself that ***nuair a bhíonn an t-ól istigh, bíonn an chiall amuigh***, and let the shame rinse away. For those who don't drink, you could replace *an t-ól* with whatever your vice is.

The Fear You'll often hear Irish people referring to themselves as having "the fear," typically the morning after a night out. "The fear" is a state of being where the memories of the night before come surging back and you're left with crippling anxiety and self-questioning. Why on earth did I say that to my boss? Why did I text my ex? Why did I eat that chicken nugget off the floor? Yep, the fear brings those questions to mind. But don't worry; like everything, the fear will pass in time.

Sláinte an bhradáin chugat BLESSING

(slawn-cha on vrah-dawn hugit hugit)

Health of a salmon upon you

The phrase ***Sláinte an bhradáin chugat*** is an Irish blessing, carrying a deeper meaning than a simple well-wishing. It's not commonly used, but when it is, it holds a special significance and serves as a reminder of Irish mythology. In Irish folklore, salmon symbolizes abundance, prosperity, and good health. The tale of *An Bradán Feasa (on brah-dawn fah-sah)* tells the story of "The Salmon of Knowledge," a mythical creature of infinite wisdom and insight. *An Bradán Feasa* was believed to bestow all the worlds' knowledge upon he who first ate this fish. This happened to be Fionn Mac Cumhaill, a legendary hunter warrior of Fenian times in Ireland. Fionn had been preparing the fish for Finegas, a wise man who had spent years searching for *An Bradán Feasa*, when he accidentally burned his thumb on the hot oil dripping from the fish. In sucking his thumb to ease the pain, he became the first to eat the fish and therefore received its bountiful knowledge. Therefore, wishing ***Sláinte an bhradáin chugat*** to someone is a wish for their overall well-being, encompassing physical health, prosperity, knowledge, and spiritual growth. It's a wish for a life as vibrant and strong as a salmon swimming upstream. You might hear this blessing at special or ceremonious life events, celebrations, religious events, or perhaps when offering support to someone facing a challenge.

Tarraingíonn scéal scéal eile PROVERB

(tah-ring-ee-uhn shkayl shkayl ehl-eh)

One story leads to another

This proverb can be viewed and applied in a number of ways. Literally translating to "One story leads to another," it refers to the chain reaction that storytelling can cause. It's no secret that the Irish people love a good story. The practice of storytelling is deep-rooted in the country's culture, and this proverb is the epitome of that sentiment. In a literal sense, when one person begins to tell a story, it can remind another of a similar story or experience that they would like to share or add to the conversation. Think of times when you've called a friend for a so-called quick catch-up, and you find yourselves in the same position hours later chatting about anything and everything, uttering phrases like "Oh, that reminds me . . ." and "I forgot to mention . . ." In a more figurative sense, ***Tarraingíonn scéal scéal eile*** is a motto to be inquisitive in life. If you follow one path, subsequent doors will likely open, taking you down a different path and leading you to discover more than what you initially anticipated. In a different context, this proverb also serves as a great motto for journalists as a reminder that there's always more to a story than what meets the eye, and if you keep digging, you're guaranteed to unearth more information.

Tír gan teanga, tír gan anam PROVERB

(teer gaan CHAN-gah, teer gawn AWN-um)

A country without a language is a country without a soul

May every Irish speaker (novice and expert alike) forever have this proverb engrained in their minds. ***Tír gan teanga, tír gan anam*** is one of the most poignant proverbs among the Irish-speaking community due to its reference to a painful history of linguistic oppression. By this point, it should be crystal clear to you that the Irish language is weaved into every strand of Irish culture, including heritage, mythology, rituals, and practice. Throughout periods of history in Ireland where *Gaeilge* was stifled, these other associated aspects of the country were also subsequently stifled. The proverb ***Tír gan teanga, tír gan anam*** urges you to reflect that a country's language is the soul of that country, and therefore, a country without a language lacks a soul. The language of a people is intertwined with who they are as a society, why they do the things they do, and why they say the things they say; this is absolutely true for the Irish people, regarding the Irish language. Although the proverb ***Tír gan teanga, tír gan anam*** serves as a painful reminder of the oppression of the Irish language and how the soul of the country was challenged, Irish speakers have claimed this proverb. It's now used as words of encouragement to continue preserving, protecting, and promoting the Irish language.

Tochas gan ingne ort CURSE

(TUCKH-iss gawn IHN-gneh urt)

May you have an itch you can't scratch

Tochas gan ingne ort is another beautiful example of an equally peculiar and petty hex in the Irish language. Unlike curses invoking physical harm or a one-way ticket to the underworld, this curse focuses on a persistent, intensely irritating, yet ultimately harmless annoyance. This curse literally translates to "An itch without fingernails upon you," but in a more figurative sense, it could be framed as "May you have an itch you can't scratch."

The exact origins of this curse are uncertain, meaning it's not known exactly who the evil genius was that first wished ***Tochas gan ingne ort*** upon an enemy. If that person were still alive today, they would definitely deserve an award for cruel creativity. Therefore, this curse was likely born from Ireland's rich oral tradition where playful curses and blessings were commonplace. ***Tochas gan ingne ort*** is not found in ancient texts, but it exists as part of the living language, passed down through generations. The image conjured is vividly unpleasant: an unbearable itch, impossible to scratch. The curse's effectiveness lies not in supernatural power, but in its ability to evoke a relatable feeling of frustration and mild discomfort. It's a curse best suited for minor annoyances and its inherent absurdity adds to its appeal. ***Tochas gan ingne ort*** serves as a reminder that even in moments of irritation, a touch of humor can help ease the tension.

Tús maith leath na hoibre PROVERB

(thoos mawh lyah nah HI-brah)

A good start is half the work

Tús maith leath na hoibre is a proverb that holds the essence of productivity at its core. Think of it the same way as you would think of the phrase "Fail to prepare, prepare to fail." This proverb literally translates to "A good start is half the work," and its sentiment is clear and applicable to many aspects of life. Whether in work, school, or personal feats, it's no surprise that adequate preparation and planning yields a smoother process and a more polished final result. So, make the to-do list, get yourself organized, and remind yourself that ***Tús maith leath na hoibre***. You can scribble this proverb in your diary or set it as a wallpaper on your phone or laptop as a gentle (yet important) reminder to yourself to start the thing that you've been putting off and get the work done. An equivalent proverb is "A stitch in time saves nine," meaning that implementing proper structure in your workflow and avoiding procrastination will yield a higher level of productivity and fewer bumps in the road down the line. ***Tús maith leath na hoibre*** is a proverb that everyone can find meaning in and make efforts to implement into various aspects of their life.

Ualach sé chapall de chré na h-úire ort CURSE

(OOL-ach shay khawp-ill deh khrey nah HOOR-eh urt)

Six horse loads of graveyard clay upon you

Proceed with caution as you read about this curse, as you would never use it in a lighthearted or playful manner. Instead, only use it on those you truly despise or hate. The curse ***Ualach sé chapall de chré na h-úire ort*** is a mouthful (it would take some practice before being able to roll it off your tongue in a fit of rage), and it translates to "Six horse loads of graveyard clay upon you." There is no alternative way to interpret this other than wishing death upon someone. It is likely that the reference to "six horse loads of graveyard clay" stems from the phrase "to be six feet under" that originated in England during the time of the bubonic plague. However, this link in numerology could be a coincidence given that *Gaeilge* is an ancient language, and this curse may predate the practice of being buried "six feet under." This curse should not be used lightly, reserved only for fierce enemies and feuds.

Yew Tree **The yew tree is native to Ireland and can be found planted in cemeteries across the island for two reasons. Reason number one is that it's an evergreen tree and was planted in sacred spaces by druids as a symbol of eternity. Reason number two is more on the practical side. The leaves of the yew tree are poisonous to livestock, particularly cattle, and therefore, they ensured graves would not be trampled on.**

7 Idioms and Colloquialisms

"Hiberno-English" refers to the English spoken in Ireland and how its linguistic patterns and characteristics have been shaped by the presence of the Irish language, *Gaeilge*. In addition to the presence of Hiberno-English in Irish people's vernacular, the island and its people yield a wide variety of wacky, beautiful, and interesting phrases and expressions. As a nation renowned for their sharp tongue and cunning wit, the Irish certainly have no shortage of lovable idioms and colloquialisms, and gaining an understanding and awareness of them is crucial to understanding the Irish tongue.

ag magadh VERBAL NOUN

(egg MAWG-ah)

messing

The Irish are renowned for being a nation of "messers," otherwise known as those who love to engage in the act of ***ag magadh***. This phrase and its equivalent English translation of "messing" refers to joking, kidding, or teasing. The Irish have an intrinsic playful banter that's reflected in their sharp-witted sense of humor and lighthearted mocking tendencies. Saying you were only ***ag magadh***, or "ah sure I was only messing," is the perfect scapegoat to justify a dig, whether it was harmless or intentionally provocative. If the other party takes offense to your taunt and the joke doesn't land in the way you anticipated, an effective way to avoid any tension is to brush it off by claiming you were only ***ag magadh***. Whether or not the other party accepts that you were in fact only ***ag magadh*** is a different story, but it's well worth the attempt as a get out of jail free card of sorts. If in the company of Irish people, it can be guaranteed that jokes and pleasantries will be exchanged back and forth and thrown around in a jesting manner, often poking fun at one another. The Irish are not shy of getting in a dig when in comfortable company, and taking offense to these digs is rarely a consequence—unless a particularly sore spot has been prodded.

ag stealladh báistí VERB

(egg SHTAHL-ah BAWSHTH-ee)

pouring rain

Given the relentless and persistent rain in Ireland, it's no surprise that the nation possesses various colorful ways to describe weather conditions, both *as Gaeilge* and in English. One of the most widely used expressions used among Irish speakers to describe heavy rain is ***ag stealladh báistí***. The *ag* in ***ag stealladh báistí*** functions as the *-ing* when preceding the verbal noun, with the verbal noun in the case of this phrase being *stealladh*, which translates to "downpour" or "gushing." Finally, *báistí* is from the word *báisteach*—meaning "rain" in the genitive case (a case that is implemented after verbal nouns). Therefore, ***ag stealladh báistí*** translates to "pouring rain." The word *báisteach* itself, meaning "rain," stems from the Middle Irish word *báitsech* and likely from the root word *baithis*, which refers to "top" or "crown." The word *as Gaeilge* for "baptism" also stems from the root word *baithis*, in reference to holy water being poured upon one's crown. Some of the Irish-English colloquialisms used to refer to heavy rain that you can hear on the streets of the island include: "lashing rain," "bucketing down," "pissing rain," "opening the heavens," "hammering," and "pelting down." See? Told you there was no shortage of colorful ways to describe the rain.

ag tabhairt amach VERB

(egg TORE-rth ah-MOCKH)

giving out; complaining; scolding someone

The Irish phrase ***ag tabhairt amach*** literally translates to "giving out"; however, its meaning in colloquial Irish is far richer than a simple act of distribution. This phrase, which is used every day by Irish people, makes no sense without an understanding of its roots in the Irish language. Therefore, ***ag tabhairt amach*** is a perfect example of Hiberno-English. When Irish people use the expression ***ag tabhairt amach*** when speaking Irish, and "giving out" when speaking English, people are often confused. In both *Gaeilge* and Irish English, ***ag tabhairt amach*** or "giving out" refers to the act of scolding, complaining, or expressing discontent. For example, a parent would be ***ag tabhairt amach*** or "giving out" to their child to discipline them for bad behavior. Similarly, a teacher might do the same to their students, or a boss to their employees. In Hiberno-English, referring to "telling someone off" as "giving out" stems wholly from the phrase ***ag tabhairt amach*** in the Irish language. As well as referring to discipline or scolding, ***ag tabhairt amach*** also refers to complaining. For example, one might be quickly prompted to "stop their giving out!" when whining. The phrase is informal and often used humorously, acknowledging the commonality of expressing dissatisfaction. It's a phrase that captures the lively nature of Irish social interactions, scoldings, and complaining.

ar eagla na heagla PHRASE

(air AHG-la nah HAHG-la)

just in case; for the fear of the fear

The Irish phrase ***ar eagla na heagla*** translates literally to "for the fear of the fear" and figuratively to "just in case" or "to be on the safe side." The phrase highlights the importance of precaution, not out of paranoia, but as a practical measure to mitigate potential risks. Rather than simply acknowledging a possibility and suffering the consequences of that possibility, ***ar eagla na heagla*** emphasizes a proactive approach and encourages you to double-check and ensure that the *eagla* is actually nothing to be feared at all! In modern and bilingual usage, ***ar eagla na heagla*** can be heard thrown in at the end of sentences to carry the sentiment of "just in case." For example, "I'll double-check I locked the door, ***ar eagla na heagla***!" or "Can you double-check that the hair straighteners are unplugged, ***ar eagla na heagla***?" It's used in everyday conversation to express the taking of extra measures, often with a touch of humor. Using ***ar eagla na heagla*** in conversation, as opposed to its English counterparts, carries a stronger sense of urgency and caution; you are taking those extra steps to ensure security out of fear, not simply "just in case."

ar luas lasrach ADVERB

(air LOO-is LAWS-ruckh)

at the speed of light

Ar luas lasrach is another beautiful phrase *as Gaeilge* that exemplifies the poetic, alliterated nature of the Irish language. This expression translates to "at the speed of light" or "at lightning speed" and carries a significant weight in Irish colloquial speech. ***Ar luas lasrach*** is not merely about literal speed; it speaks more to swiftness and urgency. The use of the adjective *lasrach*, which translates to "flaming" or "fiery," adds a vibrant, fierce imagery to the speed. It suggests not just fast movement but a sudden, explosive burst of action and energy, comparable to sparks generated as a result of intense friction. The imagery of light and flame is prevalent in Irish folklore and poetry, suggesting ancient roots. You might be on the receiving end of a demand or urgent request when hearing the phrase ***ar luas lasrach***. Picture your teacher, boss, or parental figure snapping at you: "Get that done, ***ar luas lasrach***!" A comparable word in colloquial Irish English that is used in similar context to ***ar luas lasrach*** would be "jiffy."

The Luas Ireland's only tram system can be found in the island's capital city, Dublin. It consists of two lines, the red line and the green line, which serve both the city and greater surrounding areas. The tram service is named *Luas*, which translates simply to "speed," and it is a (more often than not) effective and speedy way of navigating Dublin.

ar mhuin na muice PHRASE

(air vwin nah mwihk-eh)

on the pig's back

If you find yourself at a point where the stars seem to be aligning in your favor, ***ar mhuin na muice*** is the perfect Irish expression to use. Translating literally to "on the pig's back," this idiom's meaning and usage are nuanced and reflect a deep connection to Irish rural life and culture. The phrase doesn't refer to literally riding a pig; instead, it signifies being in a fortunate or prosperous state, enjoying good luck, or experiencing a period of success. Its origins are rooted in the importance of pigs in traditional Irish farming. A healthy, thriving pig represented wealth and prosperity for a farmer and served as a symbol of abundance and success. Being ***ar mhuin na muice*** therefore implied a position of comfort and advantage, secured by good fortune and hard work.

The idiom's usage is versatile. You might say you're ***ar mhuin na muice*** after receiving a promotion, winning a competition, or simply experiencing a run of good luck. In modern interpretations, ***ar mhuin na muice*** maintains its core meaning but also carries a playful, almost whimsical tone. It's often used informally to celebrate good fortune, expressing a sense of lightheartedness and gratitude for positive circumstances. The imagery of riding a pig adds a touch of folksy charm, making it a memorable and endearing expression within the Irish language.

ar scamall a naoi PHRASE

(air SCAWM-uhl ah knee)

on cloud nine; doing amazing

Similar to *ar mhuin na muice*, the expression ***ar scamall a naoi*** can be used at times of great delight and success. Literally translating to "on cloud nine," this is unfortunately not an ancient proverb with deep-rooted historical origins. However, it is used widely by Irish speakers and is therefore worth familiarizing yourself with if you're incorporating Irish-language expressions into your everyday life. The English phrase "on cloud nine" originated in the early twentieth century, and its eventual adoption into Irish as ***ar scamall a naoi*** is a great depiction of the adaptability of the Irish language. In fact, this expression can be viewed as the opposite of Hiberno-English. The meaning is straightforward; to be ***ar scamall a naoi*** is to be merry, elated, or in a state of blissful joy. It implies a feeling of lightness, freedom, and overwhelming positivity. The imagery of floating on a cloud, high above the world, perfectly encapsulates this sentiment, the feeling of detachment from everyday worries and concerns. In modern Irish usage, ***ar scamall a naoi*** is employed similarly to its English counterpart. It's used to describe a wide range of situations where intense happiness is felt, from romantic success, personal achievements, or simply enjoying a beautiful day. The phrase's direct translation and seamless integration into Irish demonstrate the linguistic flexibility to express universal human emotions across cultures.

bhuel INTERJECTION

(well)

well

Bhuel can be used both as a greeting and a conjunction or filler word, the same as how the word "well" functions in Irish English. Both ***bhuel*** and "well" are words that Irish speakers and Irish people often resort to and use as a filler word or a conjunction. However, note that there is one context where the word "well" is used in English that doesn't translate (pardon the pun) over to *Gaeilge*. ***Bhuel*** is not used as an adjective in the Irish language, so don't make the mistake of responding to the question "How are you keeping?" or "*Conas atá tú?*" with ***bhuel***; that's a surefire way of exposing yourself as a novice Irish speaker, but this book serves to save you from linguistically embarrassing moments like this. Instead, here are some examples of how to incorporate the word ***bhuel*** into your daily conversations. First, ***bhuel*** can be used as a greeting. This doesn't require too much explanation; simply substitute a phrase such as *Dia duit* with ***bhuel*** for a more informal approach. Second, try using ***bhuel*** as a filler word at the start of your sentences to make everything flow much smoother and mimic proficient Irish speakers. For example, "*Bhuel, conas atá tú?*," "*Bhuel, aon chraic?*," or "*Bhuel, aon scéal?*" Although in these cases the addition of ***bhuel*** is not strictly necessary, it adds an additional beat and a natural rhythm to your spoken Irish.

bím VERB

(beem)

I do be

The infamous "do be" tense in Irish English: possibly the most widely recognized example of Hiberno-English. Formally and officially referred to as the consuetudinal tense or habitual aspect, this linguistic characteristic stands as a testament to how deeply the Irish language is ingrained in the English spoken in Ireland to this day. English does not have a consuetudinal tense, but the simple present tense is used to refer to actions or happenings that occur on a regular basis, as well as usage of phrases such as "always," "usually," or "regularly." An example of this habitual aspect in English would be "I'm usually hungry first thing in the mornings." However, in both Irish and informal Irish English, there is a special grammatical clause that comes into play in contexts such as this and is unofficially referred to as the "do be" tense. In Irish, to say "I'm usually hungry first thing in the mornings," one would implement the consuetudinal tense by conjugating ***bím***. ***Bím*** consists of the root verb *bí* (to be) in the consuetudinal tense (*bíonn*, "do be"), plus the pronoun *mé* (me). Therefore, *bíonn + mé =* ***bím*** (I do be). So, in Irish, one would say *Bím ocrasach céad rud ar maidin*, which translates to "I do be hungry first thing in the mornings." The influence of the "do be" tense in Irish affects spoken English in Ireland.

bóín Dé NOUN

(boe-een djay)

ladybird; ladybug

The noun ***bóín Dé*** refers to a "ladybird" or "ladybug" and is a favorite among Irish speakers; it never ceases to delight upon unveiling its literal translation. First, *bóín* is a combination of the word *bó*, meaning "cow," followed by the diminutive suffix *-ín* (like in *a stóirín*, meaning "my little darling"). The *-ín* is added to the end of a word to signify a sense of littleness or endearment. Therefore, *bóín* in its entirety translates to "little cow." When followed by *Dé*, meaning "of God," ***bóín Dé*** therefore translates to "God's little cow." The origin of this cute critter name is said to have religious roots. The "lady" in "ladybug" refers to the Virgin Mary, who was sometimes depicted as wearing red, and the "cow" reference is believed to stem from the black dots on the insect, like a cow. However, and interestingly, the Irish language isn't the only language that can claim ownership over this endearing translation. Across the pond in Wales, *buwch goch gota* translates to "short little red cow." The Russian phrase for ladybird, *божья коровка*, yields the exact same literal translation as the Irish language: "God's little cow."

cleasaí NOUN

(clahs-ee)

chancer; a dubious person

Being known as a ***cleasaí*** in Ireland can either be regarded negatively or positively. This word translates directly to "trickster" or "con artist"; however, its colloquial Hiberno-English equivalent of "chancer" adds a layer of informal, often humorous, connotation. The term doesn't necessarily imply malicious intent; rather, it describes someone who is opportunistic, quick-witted, and adept at taking advantage of situations, often with a degree of charm or cunning nature.

In modern usage, ***cleasaí*** is used to describe someone who is shrewd, maybe a bit cheeky, and capable of getting what they want through cleverness or guile. It's a term that can be used playfully among friends, highlighting someone's opportunistic nature. However, it can also carry a more negative connotation, suggesting a lack of scruples or a tendency toward dishonesty. The context and tone when using the term ***cleasaí*** significantly impacts the interpretation. The modern understanding retains the core meaning of someone who is cunning and opportunistic, but its usage has adapted to reflect the changing social dynamics of Ireland. It remains a versatile and widely understood term, capable of conveying both admiration for someone's cleverness and disapproval of their questionable tactics. If you encounter a ***cleasaí***, you could refer to them as such: "Yer man is an awful ***cleasaí***, isn't he?"

dearg le fearg ADJECTIVE

(JAHR-ug le FAHR-ug)

angry; red with anger

The use of colors in Irish extends much further than depicting shades and tones, which can be seen exemplified in the expression ***dearg le fearg***. This Irish idiom translates literally to "red with anger." The phrase isn't merely about feeling angry; it captures the visible, almost visceral expression of said anger. The idiom's origins lie in the direct observation of human emotion; when someone is overcome with anger, their face often flushes red due to increased blood flow. This physical reaction is universally recognized, making the idiom easily understood across cultures.

An aspect that adds charm to ***dearg le fearg*** is the naturally occurring and aligning rhythm and rhyme of the expression *as Gaeilge*, which can be seen in the words *dearg* and *fearg*. In modern Ireland and among Irish speakers, ***dearg le fearg*** retains its strong visual and emotional impact. It's a testament to the power of language to convey not only the emotional state but also its physical manifestations, reflecting the close relationship between the mind and body in Irish culture. This phrase resonates with its directness and evocative imagery.

feic INTERJECTION

(feck)

feck; to see

The word ***feic***, often anglicized as "feck," is a versatile and expressive term that carries a dual meaning in the Irish language. First, ***feic*** is the verb "to see" in Irish, but in classrooms, it's sure to get students giggling. In Irish English, the word "feck," which is pronounced the same as ***feic*** (to see) in Irish, is a profanity. "Feck" is used in Ireland as a gentler, softer alternative to *that* curse word in English also beginning with the letter *f*. "Feck" is far less harsh and offensive than its counterpart and lacks the sexual connotation of the latter. It's likely that the Irish began using "feck" as an alternative because of the verb ***feic*** (to see) in Irish and the similarities between the two. So, it's clear to see why studying the verb ***feic*** (to see) gets students giggling as it is a profanity that children would often hear their parents and other adults in their surroundings saying. In casual conversation, ***feic*** or "feck" might be used as an exclamation of surprise or frustration. For example, "Feck! I forgot my wallet at home!" It can also be used as an intensifier and put into the gerund like this: "That's a fecking disaster!" Its meaning ranges from expressing mild annoyance to expressing intense frustration or anger. The strength of the word depends entirely on the tone and context in which it's used.

goille INTERJECTION

(GWILL-yah)

c'mere to me

This informal Irish expression, ***goille***, translates roughly to "come here" or more colloquially, "c'mere to me (you)." ***Goille*** is a blend that stems from that longer expression *gabh i leith*, but like many phrases, the words have mushed together over time when used in conversation. This expression is used casually in spoken Irish and would not be regarded as the standardized official way to say, "come here." Similar to English, "come here" is regarded as formal and official, but in casual spoken Irish English, "c'mere to me" is used.

The meaning of ***goille*** extends beyond a simple command, as the phrase often conveys a range of emotions and intentions beyond its literal translation. The phrase is highly contextual. It might be used affectionately to call a child or pet closer, or it could be used with a sense of urgency in a more serious situation out of frustration or urgency. ***Goille*** can also be simply used to instigate a gossip session or draw the attention of your company toward a new topic. For example, "***Goille***, I have news for you." In modern usage, ***goille*** retains its versatility and can be used to express excitement, impatience, or even mild annoyance, all depending on tone and context. The strength of the idiom lies in its ability to convey a range of emotions using a single, concise word.

íde béil NOUN

(EEDj-eh bayl)

a scolding

An ***íde béil*** is something that no one wants to find themselves on the receiving end of. This expression refers to "scolding" or "verbal abuse," or more informally, a good "telling off." The literal translation of this expression aligns with its usage. *Íde* can be translated to "ill usage" and *béil* is the noun *béal*, meaning "mouth" in the genitive case. Therefore, an ***íde béil*** is an "ill usage of the mouth." Students can be on the receiving end of an ***íde béil*** from their teachers, children from their parents, and employees from their bosses. For example, "*Fuair mé íde béil ó mo mháthair*" *(foor may ee-jah bayl oh muh waw-her)*, meaning "I got a scolding from my mother." An ***íde béil*** is often harsher and more aggressive than the act of *ag tabhairt amach* (giving out). However, ***íde béil*** and *ag tabhairt amach* generally fall under the same umbrella of scolding. Some colloquial Irish-English equivalents of ***íde béil*** are as follows:

- "Bollocking," as in "My teacher gave me an awful bollocking!"
- "To eat the head off someone," as in "My dad will eat the head off me if he finds out."

imigh leat INTERJECTION

(ih-mih lyat)

go away

When you've simply had enough of someone and need some space, feel free to hit them (linguistically, not physically) with an ***imigh leat***. The verb *imigh* is "to go away" or "to leave," and *leat* is the prepositional pronoun "with you" (a blend of *le* meaning "with" and *tú* meaning "you"). Therefore, when the pieces are all put together, ***imigh leat*** translates to "go away with you" or "leave with you." The equivalent in informal Irish English is "go away you," and even more informally "g'way will ya." ***Imigh leat*** encapsulates a range of tones, from playful dismissal to sharp rebuke, depending on context and delivery. The phrase's versatility is its strength. It can be used playfully among friends, expressing a lighthearted desire for some space or a gentle teasing. Conversely, it can be a sharp and abrupt command, conveying annoyance or frustration. The tone is entirely dependent on the context and the speaker's inflection, ranging from affectionate dismissal to outright anger.

To Hell or to Connacht "To hell or to Connacht" is an expression associated with the seventeenth-century Cromwellian conquests of Ireland and the 1652 Act for the Settlement of Ireland. This act called for Irish Catholics to be resettled in Connacht, a province to the west of Ireland, and stipulated that those who did not relocate would face death. Although this expression is linked to Oliver Cromwell, it is likely that he never uttered the words himself.

lean ort INTERJECTION

(lyan urt)

g'wan

The phrase ***lean ort*** and its colloquial Irish-English equivalent "g'wan" are integral to informal speech in Ireland. ***Lean ort*** is a combination of the verb *lean*, "to follow" or "to continue," and the prepositional pronoun *ort*, meaning "on you." Therefore, ***lean ort*** carries the sentiment of "keep going" or "go on." The phrase is used as a term of encouragement and inspiration, often in a cheering manner. Parents and coaches would be heard exclaiming a passionate "***Lean ort!***" on the sidelines of sporting events to encourage those participating. This would basically mean "Keep going! You got this!" In informal Irish English, "go on" has been shortened to "g'wan," which can then be extended to "G'wan ya good thing ya." These colloquial expressions can be used in a multitude of circumstances. Similar to ***lean ort***, "g'wan" and "G'wan ya good thing ya" will be heard on the sidelines at football matches; one might exclaim "G'wan ya good thing ya!" when spectating events such as horse racing. A heartfelt and fiery "g'wan!" can oftentimes be the final piece of encouragement that one needs to cross the finish line in triumph. Both ***lean ort*** and "g'wan" can be used socially among friends, coworkers, and family, and these expressions encapsulate the positive and supportive nature of the Irish people.

lofa ADJECTIVE

(LUH-fah)

rotten

The word ***lofa*** translates to "rotten" or "foul" in English and can be quick to roll off an Irish person's tongue in a variety of circumstances. It describes something in a state of decay or disrepair, often implying unpleasantness or unattractiveness. The word ***lofa***'s strength lies in its ability to convey a sense of disgust or disapproval with a single, evocative term, often paired with a grimace. A word similar to ***lofa*** that you will often hear within Hiberno-English is "manky." ***Lofa***'s effectiveness stemmed from the word's ability to capture a visceral reaction to something unpleasant, and in modern Irish, the word remains a common term to express disgust or disapproval. Despite the word phonetically being pleasant on the ear, while you spend time in Ireland, you should ensure you are not on the receiving end of an Irish person's use of the term ***lofa***. The word will commonly be used to describe the wet, miserable weather (unfortunately) often seen in Ireland. Picture yourself bursting in the door at home or in the office, soaked to the skin and shaking the rain off your umbrella; that is precisely the moment to implement the word ***lofa***. The word can be used on its own simply as an exclamation, accompanied with a nod or gesture to the less-than-ideal conditions outside, or used in a full sentence as "*Tá an lá lofa, nach bhfuil?*" *(taw on law luhfah nawk will)*, translating to "The day is rotten, isn't it?"

mo dhuine PHRASE

(muh ghwin-eh)

yer man / yer wan

How would you solve the case of ***mo dhuine***; who is ***mo dhuine***? To answer the question simply, or perhaps not so simply, ***mo dhuine*** can be anyone. This Irish idiom translates directly to "my person," so one might assume that it is a term used to refer to a significant other or a best friend. This phrase is comparable to "yer man" and "yer one (wan)" in Irish English. Both ***mo dhuine*** and "yer man / wan" are playful, and often vague, ways to refer to someone without explicitly naming them; the ambiguity is part of its charm, and just about anyone can be ***mo dhuine***. To best work out who is being referred to as ***mo dhuine*** or "yer man / wan" in a conversation, it's best to direct your attention toward the person who is the topic of conversation. For example, someone might say, "I saw ***mo dhuine*** in town yesterday," without needing to clarify who ***mo dhuine*** is. The listener is expected to understand from the context of the conversation. In modern Ireland, "yer man / wan" remains a popular and versatile term. It's often used humorously or affectionately, adding a casual and understated tone to conversations. The vagueness of the phrase allows for a degree of playful secrecy or avoids the need for precise identification. It's a phrase that embodies the Irish spirit of informality and shared understanding.

ná cuireadh sé ó chodladh na hóiche thú PHRASE

(naw KWUIR-uh shay oh chuhl-ah na HEE-hah hoo)

don't lose any sleep over it

This Irish idiom, ***ná cuireadh sé ó chodladh na hoíche thú***, translating literally to "let it not keep you from night's sleep" and figuratively to "don't lose any sleep over it," is a comforting reassurance, suggesting that a particular issue isn't worth the worry or stress it might cause. The matter is insignificant or temporary, and dwelling on it will only lead to unnecessary anxiety. This idiom's essence is rooted in the human experience of sleeplessness due to worry. The phrase ***ná cuireadh sé ó chodladh na hoíche thú*** directly addresses this, suggesting that the problem at hand is not significant enough to disrupt the restorative peace of sleep. This highlights the importance of perspective, prioritization, and the ability to close your eyes at night and start a new day once the sun rises. The phrase might be used to calm someone down after a minor mishap or to encourage someone not to fret over a small setback.

Sleeping with the Devil To sleep with socks on or not to sleep with socks on: a debate as old as time and one that Irish superstition may yield the answer to. As per Irish superstition, it is claimed that sleeping with your socks on means you're sleeping with the devil. Like many Irish superstitions, its origin is uncertain, but regardless, it's best to play it safe.

nathair nimhe NOUN

(NAH-her NIHV-eh)

snake

The Irish term ***nathair nimhe*** literally translates to "poisonous snake" or "venomous snake" but is used to refer to any "snake." The etymology of this phrase can be traced back to the Old Irish word *nathir*, and even further back to the Proto-Indo-European root word *nētr* meaning snake. Historically, the phrase's meaning extended beyond the literal. Snakes, particularly venomous ones, represented danger, treachery, and hidden threats. In Irish folklore, a ***nathair nimhe*** might symbolize an insidious enemy or a deceitful individual. Its use in proverbs and sayings emphasized the potential for betrayal or unforeseen harm. In modern Ireland, referring to someone as a ***nathair nimhe*** or a "snake" is the height of insult. In calling someone a ***nathair nimhe***, you are referring to them as being a slimy, deceitful character who is not to be trusted. This insult is reserved for a backstabber or someone who would be quick to betray you. Casually, one could say "he's an awful snake" about someone who's not to be trusted under any circumstances.

Saint Patrick's Snakes According to legend, St. Patrick banished all the snakes from Ireland, although snakes have never lived on the island. Imagery of the saint often depicts him accompanied by snakes or banishing them with his staff. Given that St. Patrick brought Christianity to the island, it's believed that the snakes he banished represent the eradication of pagan belief and traditions.

ní bheadh a fhios agat PHRASE

(knee veyck ah ihs aw-gut)

you wouldn't know

Ní bheadh a fhios agat and its colloquial Irish-English equivalent "you wouldn't know" or "you never know" are utilized often in informal, casual speech. This phrase functions as a vague, neutral response to a question or a statement and serves as an effective way to improve your spoken Irish and blend in seamlessly with the community. For example, if asked "Do you think the bars will be busy tonight?," you could respond with "***Ní bheadh a fhios agat***," because truly, who knows. However, depending on the tone of delivery, ***ní bheadh a fhios agat*** can be optimistic or pessimistic. Paired with a shrug of the shoulder, it implies that you don't think the bars will be busy. Paired with a grin, it insinuates that you're hoping they will be, and you're clinging onto a glimmer of possibility. In Irish English, "you wouldn't know" or "you never know" are often preceded with a casual "ah, sure," like many colloquial expressions. There are really no rules pertaining to when one can and cannot throw in an "ah, sure." Therefore, if you're visiting Ireland or among Irish company, feel free to utilize either ***ní bheadh a fhios agat*** or "ah sure, you wouldn't know" as a vague, general response to a wide variety of questions.

Níl caill ar bith orm PHRASE

(kneel cawl air bih urm)

There's not a loss on me

Using the phrase ***Níl caill ar bith orm*** or it's translation, "There's not a loss on me," is an effective way to avoid a robotic response to the question "How are you?" or "How are you getting on?" when among a crowd of Irish people. This response captures the largely positive but also avoidant nature of the Irish people. In responding "***Níl caill ar bith orm***" to the question "How are you?," you're not divulging how you *actually* are and what's going on in your life in a broader sense. It's more a blanket statement to say there's nothing too awful going on in your life at the moment, or perhaps there is but you're simply not in the mood to discuss it on a deeper level. However, one can also take the response at face value and have faith in the fact that using ***Níl caill ar bith orm*** means that there is in fact not a loss on you—there's nothing wrong and you're generally doing okay. This phrase sits more at a neutral position and swings positive, as opposed to being wholly positive. There are many alternative phrases in the Irish language that express that you're doing amazing, such as *ar scamall a naoi*.

Ó an stopfaidh tú PHRASE

(oh on stup-eh too)

Ah will ya stop

An essential Irish idiom to seamlessly step into conversation with the Irish people is ***Ó an stopfaidh tú***, translating to "Ah will ya stop." This phrase is equally as prevalent in the Irish language and informal Irish English. The instances in which you could use this phrase are limitless. Typically, ***Ó an stopfaidh tú*** is used to express disbelief, shock, or delight (there truly are no rules for this phrase). For example, you could use this as a response if someone has informed you of exciting news, such as a new job or excellent grades. In this case, the use of ***Ó an stopfaidh tú*** expresses delight and excitement to the person who has informed you of the good news. On the contrary, ***Ó an stopfaidh tú*** could be used to express shock if someone has shared a piece of juicy gossip with you. For example, "Did you hear that he cheated on his girlfriend?" with the outrightly Irish response being "***Ó an stopfaidh tú!***" If you were to pay homage to the literal translation of this phrase, it can also simply be used to implore another person to stop talking. If an outlandish suggestion has been put forth, feel free to whip out an ***Ó an stopfaidh tú*** with a discerning look on your face.

obair na gcapall NOUN

(UHB-ir na GAWP-ill)

horse's work

In the Irish language, the phrase ***obair na gcapall*** is used to refer to someone who is working extremely hard or putting in a serious shift. Literally translating to "the work of the horses" or "horse's work," this is an example of an Irish-language idiom that hasn't directly been adapted into Hiberno-English. However, the phrase "working like a Trojan," referring to the Greek tale of the Trojan horse, is an idiom largely used in Ireland but is not likely linked to the phrase ***obair na gcapall***. Another Irish colloquialism in reference to someone working hard would be "he / she / they are working like a dog," or similarly "he / she / they were worked like a dog." ***Obair na gcapall*** would have historically been used to describe intensive, laborious physical work, similar to that of farm horses. Farm horses played an integral role in the farming industry of Ireland, and it was estimated that there were over 350,000 horses working on Irish farms in 1939. A strong work ethic is highly valued in Ireland, and the majority of the nation knows how to work hard, and play even harder.

plámás | plámásaí NOUN

(plaaw-maws) | (plaw-maaws-ee)

act of flattering; flatterer

The infamous ***plámásaí***—you either love, hate, or love to hate them. The Irish word ***plámás*** refers to flattery or smooth-talking, and the Irish have cultivated and mastered this skill. The usage of the terms ***plámás*** and ***plámásaí*** (an act and a title, respectively) point to a long-standing recognition of flattery. The term doesn't carry a purely negative connotation; it can also imply charm and persuasiveness.

Historically, the word ***plámásaí*** was used to describe someone skilled in the art of persuasion, one who was renowned for often using compliments and charm to achieve their goals. This could range from charming a potential romantic partner to manipulating someone into a favorable agreement. The context often determined whether the term was used positively or negatively and would clarify the intended meaning. In Hiberno-English, these words from the Irish language are preserved but anglicized, and people will be referred to as a "plámáser" (pronounced *plaw-maws-er*).

Don't Trust the Leprechaun Although the leprechaun is now portrayed as a lovable cultural icon, its mythological origins are sinister. In Irish folklore, the leprechaun is a devilish trickster. Using the act of ***plámás***, these creatures deceived others and bartered for their freedom when captured for their treasures.

prochóg NOUN

(pruh-khoge)

kip; messy place

One must always fear the wrath of an Irish mammy (Mom), even more so if one's dwellings are in a state of being a ***prochóg***. Translating to a "messy place" or more colloquially a "kip," this word can be used to describe a house, room, or general surroundings that are in a state of utter disarray. God forbid there are visitors arriving at the house and it looks like a ***prochóg***; an Irish mammy will demand that every nook and cranny be cleaned immediately, including polishing the windows and dusting out the cupboard (because of course a cleanliness investigation is the first thing said visitors will do). In Irish English, alternatives to the word ***prochóg*** are "pigsty," the adjective "manky," or saying, "the place is in a shambles."

Hide Your Dirty Laundry Like women in cultures across the globe, Irish housewives were scrutinized for their domestic capabilities. Traditionally, the household's laundry was hung to dry on a clothesline, often to the front of the home in clear view of the village or locality. Housewives would be judged or valued based on the way in which their laundry was hung. There were expected norms to follow and unspoken rules, such as bedsheets and towels being hung to the outside of the line to hide underwear and other unmentionables.

rud a chur ar an méar fada PHRASE

(ruh a khur air on mair FAWD-ah)

to put something on the long finger

The Irish idiom ***rud a chur ar an méar fada*** translates literally to "to put something on the long finger." This idiom should be viewed in the light of its figurative context, as opposed to the literal translation, because it has nothing to do with actual fingers and their lengths. Instead, it signifies procrastination or delaying a task indefinitely. The idiom's origins are rooted in the image of a long finger, which suggests a distant, unreachable point in time. If you put something *ar an méar fada*, it implies a deliberate postponement, often without a firm commitment to completing the task in the future. It's not simply forgetting or overlooking something; it's a conscious decision to delay your responsibilities, often due to a lack of urgency or motivation. Someone might say, "I've been putting that essay *ar an méar fada*," implying that they haven't started it yet or have been delaying its completion. This phrase is often used humorously, self-deprecatingly, or even apologetically, acknowledging the delay and perhaps hinting at a lack of seriousness about the task. In modern Ireland, ***rud a chur ar an méar fada*** remains a widely used and understood idiom. It's a uniquely Irish way of expressing the common experience of putting things off with a touch of self-aware humor and cultural specificity.

sibh PRONOUN

(shiv)

you (plural)

In English, the second-person pronoun "you" is used to express both the singular and the plural form. Informally, "you" can be paired with words such as "guys" to express the plural, like in "Will I see you guys later?" Another example is the word "y'all." In the Irish language, the word ***sibh*** refers to the second-person plural. For example, "*An bhfeicfidh mé ar ball sibh?" (on vek-ee may air ball shiv)*, which translates to "Will I see you (plural) later?" The presence of the second-person plural in Irish has carried over to the English spoken in Ireland, resulting in the usage of words such as "yous," "yiz," and "ye" to refer to the plural form of "you." Although English does not inherently require alternate words to refer to a plural "you," the practice of doing so remains in Hiberno-English as a reflection of *Gaeilge* and the second-person plural ***sibh***. So, the usage of "yous," "yiz," and "ye" is widespread in Ireland with many unaware that these forms of "you" (plural), in particular "yous," are not standardized. Examples of these pronouns in use include "Have ye listened to the new album yet?" and "Did yiz see what she was wearing the other day?" Being aware of the use of the informal second-person plural in Hiberno-English is crucial to understanding casual spoken English in Ireland, and understanding that this practice reflects *Gaeilge* will earn you further brownie points.

tá a fhios agat féin PHRASE

(taw ah ihs aw-gut fayn)

you know (y'know) yourself

Tá a fhios agat féin translates directly to "you know yourself" and is an idiom used both *as Gaeilge* and in Irish English. This phrase captures the art of Irish nuance beautifully. The phrase often implies a level of familiarity between speaker and listener, suggesting a shared history or understanding that doesn't require explicit explanation. It can be used to convey a range of subtle meanings, from gentle encouragement to a hint of sarcasm or even mild rebuke. The phrase's usage is highly contextual. It can be used to gently encourage someone to make their own decision, implying that they possess the necessary knowledge or intuition. Alternatively, it can be used sarcastically to suggest that the listener should know better or to imply that their question is somewhat obvious. The idiom's enduring appeal lies in its subtle ambiguity, allowing it to function as both a comforting reassurance and a gentle nudge, depending entirely on the context and the relationship between the speaker and listener. For example, someone could ask, "How was your vacation?" with an innately Irish response being "***Tá a fhios agat féin***" or "Ah sure y'know yourself," meaning you don't need to go into the minute details of the vacation; it should be obvious what the trip entailed. Does anyone truly know what ***tá a fhios agat féin*** means? Ah sure, at the end of the day, ***tá a fhios agat féin***!

tá an ghrian ag scoilteadh na gcloch PHRASE

(taw on ghree-un egg skwuil-cheh nah gluckh)

the sun is splitting the stones

The Irish phrase ***tá an ghrian ag scoilteadh na gcloch***, translating to "the sun is splitting the stones," paints a vivid picture of intense heat. It suggests a scorching, almost unbearable level of warmth that is capable of cracking stones. The phrase is not just about a sunny day; it implies extreme heat. The phrase's origin likely stems from Ireland's experience with intense summer heat, a relatively rare but memorable occurrence in a climate often characterized by milder temperatures and extraordinarily wet days. In traditional usage, the phrase ***tá an ghrian ag scoilteadh na gcloch*** described exceptionally hot days, often with a sense of wonder or awe at the intensity of the heat. The idiom's enduring power lies in its ability to evoke a strong sensory experience, recalling the image of the sun's unrelenting power, capable of cracking even the most resistant materials. The phrase's metaphorical extension allows it to be used in a wider range of contexts, making it a versatile and memorable expression in modern Irish. This phrase also holds an almost meme-worthy status as it's so heavily taught in Irish schools and therefore often recalled when people are drawing on their *cúpla focal*.

tar éis PREPOSITION

(tar aysh)

after; just

The term ***tar éis*** in the Irish language translates to "after" and is used as a preposition in the expected way. For example, "*Feicfidh mé tar éis na hoibre thú*" *(fek-ee may tar aysh nah hi-brah hoo)*, meaning "I'll see you after work." However, the term ***tar éis*** is an integral aspect of Irish sentence structure when quantifying that something has happened in the immediate past, and it functions in a similar way to the word "just" in English. An example of ***tar éis*** being used in this context would be "*Tá mé díreach tar éis ithe*" *(taw may dee-ruk tar aysh ithe)*, which contextually translates to "I've just eaten," but literally translates to "I am directly after eating." This linguistic pattern has been adapted by Irish English speakers, and the word "after" is littered in casual conversations, making this a perfect example of Hiberno-English. Irish people will say, "I'm after seeing your friend in the shop," or "My mam is after telling me something really exciting."

An Aimsir Chaite **The past tense, *an aimsir caite (on ime-shur kaw-cha)*, is the most straightforward tense to conjugate in Irish and therefore the perfect place for beginners to start. This tense dictates that a *d* be placed before verbs that begin with a vowel, and a *séimhiú* (the letter *h*) be placed after the first letter of verbs that begin with the letters *b*, *c*, *d*, *f*, *g*, *m*, *p*, *s*, and *t*.**

timireacht NOUN

(TIM-ih-rukt)

running errands

The word ***timireacht*** refers to the act of running errands, going grocery shopping, or doing odd jobs or chores around the house. In colloquial Irish English, this is called "to do the messages." This phrase stems from a time where post offices in Ireland doubled as general stores, and therefore, going to collect the "messages," or the post, also meant picking up the groceries and necessities from the shop. Children were sent out to do the weekly shop and other odd jobs and were therefore referred to as the "messengers." So, the goods they returned home with were then called the "messages." The act of ***timireacht*** has a light, airy connotation similar to strolling around town or leisurely doing household chores with no sense of urgency. Imagine yourself sauntering around casually with your favorite beverage in hand, perhaps popping into a few shops here and there; that word is ***timireacht***.

The GPO The GPO, or General Post Office, is an iconic building located on the main street of Dublin that played an integral role in the 1916 Easter Rising. Being one of the oldest operating postal headquarters in the world, this notable structure has witnessed times of rebellion and political strife. In fact, the bullet marks from battles past can still be seen on its walls today.

togha ADJECTIVE / INTERJECTION

(thoow)

sound

The Irish word ***togha*** is an informal term translating to "sound," "okay," or "grand." Both the word ***togha*** itself and its various equivalents in Irish English are versatile words that are used to express approval and satisfaction. The term is used in casual conversation, generally among friends and family, rather than in formal settings. For example, "I'll see you later!" with an appropriate response being ***togha*** or "sound," meaning "okay" or "no problem." ***Togha*** can also be used as an adjective and a common term of approval. If someone is referred to as being ***togha*** or "sound," it means they are generally a decent person. It is likely that the usage of the word "sound" in this context originates from the concept of someone being "of sound mind," meaning that they are quite steady and stable. For example, calling someone "sound out" or referring to them as being "awful sound" is a widely used compliment among Irish people. The informal nature of the word ***togha*** gives a sense of warmth and genuineness; it's an extremely useful and versatile term in either Irish or Hiberno-English when attempting to dip your toes into the mannerisms of speech. The word ***togha***'s adaptability reflects the Irish tendency toward lively and expressive speech.

Further Reading and Listening

Books

A Treasury of Irish Fairy and Folk Tales.
By Various. Published by Barnes & Noble.
A collection of over two hundred Irish folk stories and fairytales.

Gaeilge Gan Stró: Beginners Level.
By Éamonn Ó Dónaill.
A language course for those who know no Irish or simply a few phrases.

Motherfoclóir.
By Darach Ó Séaghdha.
A contemporary approach to the Irish language.

Thirty-Two Words for Field.
By Manchán Magan.
Explore the roots of the Irish language in nature.

Podcasts

***Bitesize Irish Podcast* hosted by Eoin Ó Conchúir.**
A discussion podcast for Irish language learners.

➤ **www.bitesize.irish/bitesize-irish-podcast/**

***Dúchas* hosted by Cúán de Búrca and Cían Mac Coisteala.**
A podcast in Irish that discusses all things Irish folklore, mythology, and superstitions.

➤ **https://podcasts.apple.com/ie/podcast/d%C3%BAchas/id1817816186**

***Gaeilge Weekly* by Learn Irish Online.**
A podcast offering bilingual, simpler Irish, and fluent Irish episodes.

➤ **https://open.spotify.com/show/2jaG6cYslU0a70xvaL1zBE**

***How to Gael* hosted by Doireann Ní Ghlacáin, Louise Cantillon, and Síomha Ní Ruairc.**
A bilingual (Irish and English) podcast that discusses what it means to be a *Gael*.

➤ **www.howtogael.com**

TV, Radio, and Social Media

Raidió Rí-Rá.
An Irish-language youth radio station comprising of chart music and a variety of special guests and interviews.

➤ **https://www.rrr.ie**

TG4 Player.
Watch a variety of Irish-language shows and movies, live or on demand.

➤ **www.tg4.ie**

Search the following hashtags on all social media platforms to discover Irish-language content creators: #gaeilge #gaeltok #gaeilgeoir #irishlanguage

About the Author

Laura Pakenham is a TikTok creator and online educator, promoting the learning of *Gaeilge* to her followers through tips and Irish-language videos. She has worked as a presenter on TG4, Ireland's first Irish-language TV station, which reaches an average of 1.2 million people in the Republic of Ireland weekly. Laura anchored *Nuacht Cúla4*, a daily news program for young people. Follow her at @laurajpakenham.